Current Controversies in Metaphysics

Elizabeth Barnes's Current Controversies in Metaphysics features ten essays by leading experts on some of the most central debates in the field. It is an excellent addition to Routledge's Current Controversies series, and a valuable resource for anyone looking to find a sophisticated yet accessible overview of key conversations now taking place within this core area of philosophy.

—Michael Rea, University of Notre Dame

This book showcases a range of views on topics at the forefront of current controversies in the field of metaphysics. The contributors include some of the most important philosophers currently writing on these issues. The questions and philosophers are:

- Are there any individuals at the fundamental level? / (1) Shamik Dasgupta (2) Jason Turner
- Is there an objective difference between essential and accidental properties? / (1) Meghan Sullivan (2) Kris McDaniel and Steve Steward
- Are there any worldly states of affairs? / (1) Daniel Nolan (2) Joseph Melia
- Are there any indeterminate states of affairs? / (1) Jessica Wilson (2) Elizabeth Barnes and Ross Cameron
- Do ordinary objects exist? / (1) Trenton Merricks (2) Helen Beebee

Editor Elizabeth Barnes guides readers through these controversies (all published here for the first time), with a synthetic introduction and succinct abstracts of each debate.

Elizabeth Barnes is Associate Professor of Philosophy at the University of Virginia. She is the author of *The Minority Body* (2016) and has published in *Nous, Mind*, and *Ethics*.

Current Controversies in Philosophy

In venerable Socratic fashion, philosophy proceeds best through reasoned conversation. **Current Controversies in Philosophy** provides short, accessible volumes that cast a spotlight on ongoing central philosophical conversations. In each book, pairs of experts debate four or five key issues of contemporary concern, setting the stage for students, teachers and researchers to join the discussion. Short chapter descriptions precede each chapter, and an annotated bibliography and study questions conclude each debate. In addition, each volume includes both a general introduction and a supplemental guide to further controversies. Combining timely debates with useful pedagogical aids allows the volumes to serve as clear and detailed snapshots, for all levels of readers, of some the most exciting work happening in philosophy today.

Series Editor:

John Turri
University of Waterloo

Volumes in the Series Published:

Current Controversies in Bioethics
S. Matthew Liao and Collin O'Neil

Current Controversies in Philosophy of Film
Katherine Thomson-Jones

Current Controversies in Political Philosophy
Edited by Thom Brooks

Current Controversies in Virtue Theory
Edited by Mark Alfano

Current Controversies in Epistemology
Edited by Ram Neta

Current Controversies in Experimental Philosophy
Edited by Edouard Machery and Elizabeth O'Neill

Current Controversies in Philosophy of Mind
Edited by Uriah Kriegel

Praise for the Series:

"This series constitutes a wonderful addition to the literature. The volumes reflect the essentially dialectical nature of philosophy, and are edited by leading figures in the field. They will be an invaluable resource for students and faculty alike."
Duncan Pritchard, *The University of Edinburgh*

Current Controversies in Metaphysics

Edited by
Elizabeth Barnes

Routledge
Taylor & Francis Group

NEW YORK AND LONDON

First published 2017
by Routledge
711 Third Avenue, New York, NY 10017

and by Routledge
2 Park Square, Milton Park, Abingdon, Oxon, OX14 4RN

Routledge is an imprint of the Taylor & Francis Group, an informa business

© 2017 Taylor & Francis

Library of Congress Cataloging in Publication Data
Names: Barnes, Elizabeth B., 1938– editor.
Title: Current controversies in metaphysics / edited by Elizabeth Barnes.
Description: 1 [edition]. | New York : Routledge-Taylor & Francis, 2016.
Identifiers: LCCN 2016024034 | ISBN 9780415855655 (hardback) |
    ISBN 9780203735602 (e-book)
Subjects: LCSH: Metaphysics.
Classification: LCC BD111 .C87 2016 | DDC 110—dc23
LC record available at https://lccn.loc.gov/2016024034

ISBN: 978-0-415-85565-5 (hbk)
ISBN: 978-0-203-73560-2 (ebk)

Typeset in Minion
by Apex CoVantage, LLC

Contents

Contributors

Elizabeth Barnes is Associate Professor of Philosophy at the University of Virginia. She is the author of *The Minority Body* (2016) and has published in *Nous, Mind,* and *Ethics.*

Helen Beebee is Professor of Philosophy at University of Manchester. She is the author of *Hume on Causation* (Routledge, 2006), and has published in *Philosophical and Phenomenological Research* and *Proceedings of the Aristotelian Society.*

Ross Cameron is Associate Professor of Philosophy at University of Virginia. He is the author of *The Moving Spotlight* (2015) and has published in *Philosophical Perspectives, Philosophy and Phenomenological Research,* and *Nous.*

Shamik Dasgupta is Associate Professor of Philosophy at Princeton University. He is co-editor of *Current Controversies in Philosophy of Science* (Routledge, forthcoming) and has published in *Nous, The Philosophical Review,* and *Philosophical Perspectives.*

Kris McDaniel is Professor of Philosophy at Syracuse University. He is the author of *The Fragmentation of Being* (Oxford University Press, forthcoming), and has published in *Philosophical Quarterly, Philosophical Studies,* and *Nous.*

Joseph Melia is a Senior Research Fellow at Oxford University. He is the author of *Modality* (2003).

Trenton Merricks is Professor of Philosophy at University of Virginia. He is the author of *Propositions* (2015), and has published in *Journal of Philosophy*, *Mind*, and *Analysis*.

Daniel Nolan is McMahon-Hank Professor of Philosophy at the University of Notre Dame. He is the author of *Topics in the Philosophy of Possible Worlds* Routledge 2002), *David Lewis* (Routledge 2014), and has published in *Nous*, *Philosophy and Phenomenological Research*, and *Australasian Journal of Philosophy*, amongst others.

Steve Steward is a postdoctoral research fellow at the University of Southampton, UK. He has published in *Synthese* and *The Leibniz Review*.

Meghan Sullivan is Associate Professor of Philosophy at University of Notre Dame. She has published in *Nous*, *Ethics*, and *Philosophical Studies*.

Jason Turner is Associate Professor of Philosophy at University of Arizona. He is the author of *The Facts in Logical Space: A Tractarian Ontology* (2016) and has published in *Philosophical Quarterly*, *Faith and Philosophy*, and *Australasian Journal of Philosophy*.

Jessica Wilson is Associate Professor of Philosophy at University of Toronto. She has published in *Nous*, *Philosophical Quarterly*, *British Journal for Philosophy of Science*, and *Philosophers' Imprint*.

Introduction

1. Current Controversies in Metaphysics

Metaphysics is a large, somewhat unruly area of philosophy. And while the boundaries of most any philosophical topic are amorphous and vague, this is perhaps especially (and ironically) true of metaphysics. With that in mind, I want to begin by saying what this book is *not* going to cover.

There many areas of metaphysics in which metaphysical questions are embedded in wider conversations. For example, debates about the metaphysics of race and gender are part of ongoing discussions in philosophy of race and feminist philosophy, debates about the metaphysics of science are situated in the wider context of philosophy of science, debates about the metaphysics of moral properties are an integral part of metaethics, and so on. For most any thing, you can do metaphysics about that thing. And philosophers across a huge range of philosophical conversations—whether by intention or by accident—often end up doing metaphysics of some form or other.

There are also, however, a range of conversations which are less integrated into other areas of philosophy and which, for better or worse, are primarily of interest to those who self-describe as 'metaphysicians'. The topics covered in this volume are drawn from this range of conversations. That's not at all to say that the metaphysics of race and gender, moral properties, belief, propositions, etc. don't also deserve the label 'current controversies in metaphysics'. It's just that they could also easily deserve other labels (they are also current controversies, for example, in the philosophy of race and gender, metaethics, philosophy of mind and perception, and philosophy of language, respectively). Given this volume's role in the wider series of *Current Controversies* volumes, I decided to focus it specifically on topics that are a central part of mainstream analytic metaphysics, but are not widely discussed—or at least not widely discussed in the way metaphysicians discuss them—elsewhere.

This volume also doesn't canvas any of the debates central to the ongoing conversation in meta-metaphysics. There's no specific discussion of grounding, priority, dependence, the in virtue of relation, and so on. That's mostly just a matter of editorial preference. Those debates are all, without doubt, very current controversies in metaphysics. But I wanted this volume to highlight all the interesting work being done in good, old-fashioned first-order metaphysics. Grounding and friends can sit this one out.

Okay, so enough about what this volume *doesn't* cover. Obviously, no collection of six topics will give you an overview of an entire field—especially a field as big as metaphysics. The goal of this volume, rather, is to showcase the *kinds* of conversations being had in contemporary metaphysics and *how* those conversations are being carried out.

We begin by examining a central issue in the metaphysics of objects. We tend to think of the world as containing lots of individual objects—the Eiffel Tower, my dog, this book, etc. But is this ordinary way of thinking of the world a good way of thinking about what the world is *really* like? Jason Turner and Shamik Dasgupta debate this question—the question of whether there are individuals at the fundamental level. Dasgupta construes this question as boiling down to the question (posed by Robert Adams) of whether the world is constituted by purely qualitative facts. Turner—like most metaphysicians, including Adams himself—argues that it is not. Dasgupta defends the view—which he calls 'qualitativism' and contrasts to 'individualism'—that it is. Both Dasgupta and Turner agree on a basic premise: since Newton, scientists have privileged a qualitative description of the world. (That is, explanation in science tends to focus more on which specific qualities are had by individuals, rather than which specific individuals instantiate those qualities.) Dasgupta uses this premise as an argument that individuals themselves are explanatorily idle, and therefore shouldn't be considered fundamental. Turner pushes back against this, arguing that explanatory appeal to individuals might be ineliminable.

From the metaphysics of objects, we then turn to the metaphysics of properties. There is a tendency to view some properties as having a particularly special connection to their bearers—they are part of *what it is* to be that particular thing, or they are properties which that thing couldn't have lacked. But there is a longstanding debate in metaphysics over whether this distinction tracks anything objective. That is, there is a debate over whether the difference between properties which are had *essentially* and properties which are had *accidentally* is a real one. Meghan Sullivan considers the view—which she labels 'hardcore essentialism'—that there is at least one object, O, and one property, P, such that if O exists, O must have P, where P is a qualitative property which objects can fail to instantiate. She argues against this view, making the case that it does no substantial explanatory work. Kris McDaniel and Steve Steward respond by disputing the way she frames the issue. The main motivation for essentialism is not, they argue, the explanatory work it can do in philosophical theories, but rather the central place it holds in our basic modal beliefs. If we can't accept that we could have been poached eggs or pieces of sand in a vast desert, then hardcore essentialism is true.

We then move on to the metaphysics of the relationship *between* objects and properties. Particular things instantiate particular qualities. For example, the flower sitting in a vase on the table in front of me is yellow. But arguably neither the existence of the flower nor the existence of the yellowness explain why it's true that this particular flower is yellow; the flower could've been a different colour, and yellowness could've existed without being exemplified by this flower. Daniel Nolan argues that there is a straightforward solution to this puzzle. We should believe, not merely in the existence of the flower and the property of being yellow, but also in the particular state of affairs of *the flower being yellow*. Metaphysicians have often found commitment to states of affairs unparsimonious, but Nolan argues that these parsimony worries are misguided. Joseph Melia, in contrast, argues that states of affairs are ontologically superfluous. We don't need to believe in them, he argues, to explain the truth of things such as 'The flower is yellow'.

Continuing the discussion of states of affairs, we then consider the question of whether states of affairs could be indeterminate. Indeterminacy is generally thought to be a feature of how we represent the world, rather than how the world is in and of itself. Suppose the flower on my table is a dusky shade of yellowish orange. There may simply be no fact of the matter about whether the flower is (determinately) yellow. But that's typically understood as a matter of how we describe the situation, rather than some deep metaphysical fact about the situation itself. The flower is (determinately) some colour or other. But perhaps there's no fact of the matter about whether that colour falls under the extension of the English predicate 'is yellow' in this particular context, given the somewhat loose and imprecise way in which speakers of English use the word 'yellow'. There might be some cases of indeterminacy, though, where we're tempted to think that the indeterminacy isn't explained—or isn't wholly explained—simply by how we use language or represent things. Consider, for example, a case where we think it's indeterminate whether a foetus is a person. A realist about persons won't be happy with the claim that facts about persons are simply determined by how speakers of English use the word 'person', but might likewise think it's implausible that there is a sharp cut-off, in the gradual development of a foetus, between the stages where it is not a person and the stages where it is. What would it mean, then, to say that it is *metaphysically indeterminate* whether the foetus is a person? Jessica Wilson, Ross Cameron, and I all agree that the idea of metaphysical indeterminacy is coherent, but we disagree about how it should be interpreted. Wilson argues that commitment to metaphysical indeterminacy is commitment to indeterminate states of affairs—Cameron and I deny this.

Finally, we conclude by examining the metaphysics of ordinary objects. Metaphysicians, including those featured in this book, spend a lot of time arguing about the existence and nature of a rather esoteric class of entities—fundamental objects, properties, states of affairs, etc. But what about ordinary, everyday objects—objects such as tables, trees, and computers? What might the metaphysician have to offer for our understanding of such things? Trenton Merricks defends the radical view that the lesson of metaphysical inquiry regarding most ordinary objects should be that, in fact, there are no such things. That is, the things we typically think of as 'objects' don't really exist. Merricks argues for this by claiming that such entities, if they existed, would be causally redundant—there is nothing they do which cannot be explained by their simpler parts, and so (a qualified version of) Ockham's Razor demands we reject ontological commitment to them. Helen Beebee denies Merricks's claim that we have no good philosophical reason to believe in such entities, making a case that they do important explanatory work in our philosophical theories that is not equivalent to what is explained by their more basic parts.

These debates offer a sample of the kinds of questions metaphysicians are currently engaged in. More importantly, they give a good representation of the way these debates are often carried out. Taken together, they can give a small window into the current controversies (many of which have been 'current' since the pre-Socratics) in metaphysics.

PART I

Are There Any Individuals at the Fundamental Level?

CHAPTER 1

Can We Do Without Fundamental Individuals? Yes

SHAMIK DASGUPTA

'Is the world . . . constituted by purely qualitative facts?' So asked Adams (1979: 5). He was inclined to think not, and many share his view.[1] In contrast, I am inclined to think that it is. Here I explain why I think this (section 2), explore what kinds of qualitative facts constitute the world (section 3), discuss how other facts emerge from this qualitative basis (section 4), and outline applications of this view in the philosophy of physics (section 5).

1. Qualitativism versus Individualism

The issue is whether 'the world' is 'constituted by purely qualitative facts'. By 'the world', let us restrict ourselves to *material reality*, putting aside numbers and spirits and other intangibles. So the issue is whether *it* is constituted by purely qualitative facts. But what is a *qualitative fact*? And what does it mean for the world to be *constituted* by such things?

Start with qualitative facts. In contrast to individualistic facts, which concern particular individuals, qualitative facts make no mention of any particular individual. A little more precisely, a fact is *individualistic* iff whether it obtains depends on how things stand with a particular individual (or individuals), and *qualitative* otherwise.[2] By 'individuals' I mean what in ordinary English we call 'things'—e.g. apples, alligators, atoms, and so on.

We express individualistic facts with directly referring expressions, e.g.:

That (pointing at a particular apple) is juicy.
Obama is the president.

And in first-order logic, we regiment our talk of individualistic facts with constants, e.g.:

Fa
Rab
a≠b

In contrast, examples of qualitative facts include:

Someone is the president,
Orange is more similar to red than to blue, and
Redness and roundness are co-instantiated

since whether these obtain does not depend on how things stand with any particular individual. Perhaps the first depends on there being *someone individual or other* who is the president, but it is qualitative because it does not depend on any particular person being the president. Likewise with the third.[3]

We can express some qualitative facts with quantifiers, e.g.:

$$(\exists x)Fx$$
$$(\exists x)(Px \, \& \, (\forall y)(Py \supset x = y))$$

so long as the predicates F and P are understood to express qualitative properties. And what is a qualitative property? Roughly, one that does not concern any particular individual. The property of being juicy is qualitative. In contrast, the property of being Kripke, and the property of being Obama's sister, are both non-qualitative.

This is not to say that all qualitative facts are expressed with quantifiers. We will encounter other kinds of qualitative facts in due course. Indeed, some think that the example above concerning orange is one.

Adams's question was whether the world is *constituted by* qualitative facts. What does this mean? An affirmative answer presumably yields the following picture: that at rock bottom there are purely qualitative facts, and the individualistic facts are somehow 'fixed' or 'determined' by, and are 'nothing over and above', that qualitative basis. As the metaphor goes, all God had to do when making the world is fix the qualitative facts, and then Her work was done.

But how should these metaphors and pictures be understood? There are a number of approaches, but the one I use here focuses on whether individualistic facts *hold in virtue of* qualitative facts.[4]

The notion of one fact's holding in virtue of others sometimes goes by the name of 'ground'. To say that X holds in virtue of Y (or is 'grounded in' Y) is to say that Y explains X, in a particular sense of the word 'explains'. To illustrate, imagine going to a cricket match and asking why there is a cricket match occurring. A causal answer might describe a sequence of events that led up to the match: two teams agreed to play, arrangements were made, etc. But another answer explains what it is about the event that makes it count as a cricket match in the first place. Presumably the answer is that it is a cricket match *in virtue of* what various people are doing, e.g. throwing and hitting a ball in accordance with various laws, and so on. Explanations of this second sort are called 'grounding' or 'in virtue of' or 'constitutive' explanations. This is only the briefest of illustrations; for more clarification of the notion, see Fine (2001, 2012), Rosen (2010), Schaffer (2009), and Trogdon (2013b).

So I interpret Adams's question to be one of grounds, of whether individualistic facts are grounded in qualitative ones. Let *qualitativism* be the view that they are. And let *individualism* be the view that the order of explanation goes the other way: that qualitative facts are grounded in individualistic ones.[5]

Thus, according to individualism, the fundamental facts of the world are facts about how various *individuals* are propertied and related. Perhaps they include the fact that a particular individual *A* is red and round. No doubt a variety of qualitative facts also obtain in this situation, e.g. that *something* is red and round, and perhaps that redness and roundness are co-instantiated. But the individualist says that they hold in virtue of the individualistic fact. In contrast, the qualitativist says that the fundamental facts about the situation are various qualitative facts, and *they* explain why the individual *A* is both red and round. On this view, the fundamental facts themselves make no mention of the individual *A*.

It is important not to confuse qualitativism with *anti-haecceitism*, the modal thesis that there can be no individualistic differences between possible worlds without a qualitative difference.[6] To be sure, qualitativism does *imply* anti-haecceitism, and does so thanks to the general principle that grounds necessitate what they ground. More precisely, this principle (which I assume here) is:

Necessitation: If some facts, the Xs, ground Y, then necessarily if the Xs obtain then Y obtains too.[7]

But the reverse is not the case: anti-haecceitism does not imply qualitativism. If you are an anti-haecceitist this might be because you are a qualitativist, but it might instead be because you are an individualist with independent views about the workings of *de re* modality (such as counterpart theory) that imply anti-haecceitism—Lewis (1986) was arguably an anti-haecceitist of this latter type. Or it might even be because you are an individualist who also holds the Spinozistic view that all truths are necessary, so that anti-haecceitism is trivially true!

2. Why Qualitativism?

Individualism is (at least initially) a seductive view: it is natural to think that the most fundamental facts of the world concern how a variety of individuals are propertied and related. But I favour qualitativism. Why?

Some argue that qualitativism is the simpler and more parsimonious view. Thus, Paul (2012) says that her own version of qualitativism allows us to 'characterize the structure of reality *while maximizing ontological parsimony*' (p. 241, my emphasis). There may be merits to parsimony, but I will not lean on this consideration here.

Instead, I reject individualism because if there were individualistic facts with no qualitative grounds, the individuals they involve—call them 'primitive individuals'—would be *undetectable* and *physically redundant*. What does this mean? Let me outline the rough idea here (though see Dasgupta [2009] for more details).

Starting with the charge of undetectability, the idea is that a primitive individual is 'hidden' behind its qualities. We can detect those qualities and come to know that *something or other* has them, but according to individualism there is a *further fact of the matter* as to which individual it is, and I claim that this further fact is epistemically inaccessible. After all, if two situations were qualitative duplicates—that is, if they contained the same number of primitive individuals propertied and related in *exactly* the same way, so that they differed *only* in which primitive individuals lie behind the qualities—you would never tell them apart. This idea that primitive individuals are 'hidden' extends at least back to Locke—who described them as 'unknown support of those qualities'—and through Russell—who called them an 'unknown something' and said that they 'cannot be defined or recognized or known'.[8]

What about the charge of physical redundancy? Well, imagine a closed physical system composed of primitive individuals propertied and related in various ways. How it behaves over time depends *only* on qualitative facts about it, not on those further facts about which primitive individuals lie behind those properties and relations. To see this, note that a different closed system that starts off as a qualitative duplicate—i.e. differing *only* in which primitive individuals it contains—would behave identically. So the particular primitive individuals that populate the system make no difference to how it evolves. As it might be put, the physics is 'blind' to the primitive individuals themselves and 'cares' only about the qualitative facts about the system.

The reasoning here is designed to emulate reasoning from physics, in which it is commonplace to reject undetectable and redundant structure. The paradigm example of such reasoning concerns velocity. Start by distinguishing *absolute* from *relative* velocity: your relative velocity is your velocity relative to another material body—e.g. 30 mph *relative to the road*—while your absolute velocity (if there is such a thing) is how fast you are 'really' going, independent of any material reference point.

It is orthodoxy amongst physicists and philosophers of physics to think that there is no such thing as absolute velocity, precisely because if there were it would be undetectable and physically redundant. To see (roughly) why it would be undetectable, consider an isolated physical system of material bodies in motion. And consider a 'boosted' system that differs *only* in that the entire system is unfolding while in smooth motion relative to the first—say, 5 mph to the north. By construction, the only differences between the two systems are facts about the absolute velocities of their constituents. If there really is such a thing as absolute velocity, the two systems are genuinely distinct. But note that they are *indistinguishable*: they look (and smell and taste) exactly the same. Just recall your experiences on trains: when the train is moving smoothly, happenings within the train look exactly as they would if the train were stationary. So if you were confined to one of the systems, you would never be able to work out what anything's absolute velocity is. You could never tell whether the centre of mass of the system is at rest or in smooth motion, since it would look the same either way. In this sense, absolute velocity is undetectable.

It is also physically redundant. For consider two isolated physical systems that start out alike in all respects except that one is in smooth motion relative to the first. It turns out that, according to all our best physical theories, as they evolve, they will *always* be alike in all respects except that one is in smooth motion relative to the first. So the particular absolute velocities of things (that differ between the two systems) make no difference to how a system evolves.[9] The physics is in this sense 'blind' to absolute velocity and 'cares' only about the other facts that the two systems share.

So if absolute velocity and primitive individuals were real, they would both be undetectable and redundant in the same sense. Just as systems differing only in facts about absolute velocity are indistinguishable, so too are qualitatively identical systems that differ only in which primitive individuals lie behind the qualities. And just as the particular absolute velocities of things make no difference to how a system evolves, so too the particular primitive individuals that populate the system make no difference either.

It is commonplace to think that this is a serious mark against the view that absolute velocity is real. On pain of inconsistency, we should think that this is a serious mark against the view that primitive individuals are real, i.e. a serious mark against individualism. It does not yet follow that we should certainly reject individualism. That depends on whether there is a good enough qualitativist theory to endorse instead. But we will come to that: for now, the point is that positing primitive individuals is as serious a vice as positing absolute velocity.

There is much more to say about this idea that we should reject undetectable and redundant structure—the above is just an outline. I discuss the reasoning in detail in Dasgupta (2016), where I argue that the charge of unde-tectability is doing most of the work. In contrast, Baker (2010) argues that the charge of redundancy is more important. And both charges are intimately related, so another view is that they are ultimately the same thing. But I leave these difficult questions for another time—the above gloss is good enough to be getting on with.

3. Qualitative Structures

Suppose these considerations lead us to suspect that the fundamental facts are all qualitative. We then face two questions: (i) What kinds of qualitative facts are fundamental, and (ii) How do they ground individualistic facts? Without answers, we have no particular qualitativist view in hand, just some vague idea that some such view is likely true.

Start with the first question. Perhaps the most well-known qualitativist view is the traditional *bundle theory*, according to which the fundamental facts about the world concern which qualitative properties are 'compresent'. Thus, if a particular individual is red and round, the bundle theory says that the fundamental fact about the situation is that redness and roundness are com-present. Indeed, the bundle theorist *identifies* individuals with maximal sets of compresent properties.

The standard objection is that this view cannot make sense of symmetric situations. Consider the 'Max Black' world, a world containing just two quali-tatively identical iron spheres—each of exactly the same shape, colour, mass, etc.—2 miles apart. According to the bundle theory, each sphere is identified with the very same set of compresent properties—which is to say that the spheres are not distinct and there is only *one* of them after all.[10]

The objection does not depend on which kinds of qualitative properties are compresent. If the bundle theorist says that only *monadic* and *intrinsic* properties are compresent, she will identify each sphere with the set {spheri-cal, brown, . . .}. If she allows that *relations* can also be compresent, she will identify each with the set {spherical, brown, 2 miles from, . . .}. Either way, the spheres share exactly the same qualitative properties, so the bundle theory identifies them.

The standard responses concede that the bundle theorist cannot make sense of *two* such spheres, but argue that she can make sense of *one* sphere that is 2 miles from itself. The hope is to make *some* sense, if not perfect sense, of symmetric situations.[11] I find none of these responses satisfying, but this is not the time to argue the point. Let me instead develop a less familiar idea, namely that there is no need for the qualitativist to be a bundle theorist in the first place: there are other qualitativist views that can easily make perfect sense of symmetric situations.

This might sound surprising, for the bundle theory is often presumed to be the qualitativist's only option—Adams (1979) presumes as much, insofar as it is the only qualitativist view he considers. Thus, the objection from symmetric situations is often considered qualitativism's death-knell. But this is all a mistake. Qualitativism, remember, is the view that individualistic facts are explained in terms of qualitative ones. The bundle theory tried to implement this by constructing each individual out of qualitative properties. But another approach is to bypass the construction of each individual and simply find a qualitative characterization of the entire situation. Call this approach *generalism*.[12]

There are many ways to implement this approach, but let me outline just two: *quantifier generalism* (which I am inclined to reject) and *algebraic generalism* (which I prefer). To see the idea behind quantifier generalism, note that the Max Black world can be characterized qualitatively like so:

(*) $(\exists x)(\exists y)(x \neq y$ & x is F & y is F & x is 2 miles from y)

where 'F' expresses the intrinsic qualitative nature of each sphere. This is a purely qualitative fact: whether it holds does not depend on how things stand with any particular individual. So the quantifier generalist says that this is the most fundamental qualitative fact of a Max Black world. More generally, she says that the fundamental facts are quantified facts that we express in first-order logic without constants.

Against quantifier generalism, one might argue that it is *analytic*, or perhaps *essential*, of the existential quantifier that existential facts hold in virtue of their instances. For example, suppose something is red. Then the idea is that it is analytic or essential of the existential quantifier that, given any red object x, something is red because x is red. Both claims—that this is analytic, and that it is essential—have some plausibility, and neither is *obviously* false.[13] So this is a potential consideration against quantifier generalism. The consideration might also be developed without appeal to analyticity or essence. Perhaps it is enough if the main idea—that existential facts hold in virtue of their instances—is central to our 'web of belief'.

However it is developed, note that this consideration does not tell against qualitativism writ large. The thought is not that the instances must be fundamental. The thought just concerns quantified facts—that they cannot be fundamental. Even if the qualitativist agrees that quantified facts hold in virtue of their instances, she might insist that the instances are in turn grounded in some other qualitative matter. Indeed, this is my preferred view, as will become clear.

Some say (in conversation) that this consideration against quantifier generalism is unconvincing. If they are right, qualitativists such as myself should welcome the result! But Russell (manuscript) has developed the consideration into a rigorous argument against quantifier generalism, and I have yet to see a quantifier generalist respond.

Personally, I am uncertain about the matter.[14] But uncertainty is motivation enough to explore other approaches. Ideally, an alternative approach will make sense of the full range of situations that a quantifier generalist can, without taking quantified facts to be fundamental.

In Dasgupta (2009), I outlined an approach of this kind using the resources of algebraic logic. This is *algebraic generalism*. Like the bundle theory, this view starts with a domain of qualitative properties. But unlike in the bundle theory, the fundamental facts do not just concern which properties are compresent. Instead, algebraic generalism allows for more complex ways in which the properties can be 'stitched together'.

How does this work? I refer the reader to Dasgupta (2009) for details, but here is the rough idea. Suppose that one's initial domain of properties includes the property R of being red, the property G of being green, and the relation L of loving. One then introduces various operations by which complex properties can be constructed. Two operations are & and ~, which take properties and yield their conjunctions and negations, respectively. So (R & G) is the property of being red and green, and ~R is the property of being not red. Another operation, σ, is permutative: if L is the relation that we ordinarily think of being instantiated by the pair $<x, y>$ iff x loves y, then σL is the relation that we ordinarily think of being instantiated by $<x, y>$ iff y loves x. Thus (L & ~σL) is the relation of loving unrequitedly. Two other permutative operations are also used.

The final operation, c, is known as 'cropping'. Intuitively, when applied to a property, it says that one of its argument places is filled. Thus cL is the 1-place property of being loved, i.e. the property that we ordinarily think of being instantiated by x iff someone loves x. Applying c once more then gives ccL, the 0-place property—perhaps better called a state of affairs—of love occurring, a state that we would ordinarily describe as the state of someone loving someone.[15]

In this way, the properties are stitched together to construct states of affairs. The fundamental facts of the world then concern which of these states obtain.

The operations just described are designed to mimic the workings of first-order logic without constants. Because of this, the algebraic generalist can construct *any* state of affairs that can be expressed in first-order logic without constants: she can use the operations to stitch together a state that characterizes the situation exactly.[16] So, just as the quantifier generalist can make perfect sense of a Max Black world, so too can the algebraic generalist: according to her, it is a world in which the fundamental fact is that a certain state of affairs obtains (a state that consists of various qualitative properties stitched together in a certain way). Thus, like the quantifier generalist, the algebraic generalist has no problem making sense of symmetric situations.

The advantage of algebraic generalism is that, unlike in quantifier generalism, there is little temptation to think that the facts she claims to be fundamental *must* hold in virtue of individualistic facts. For her, ontology is clear: there are just properties, stitched together by the operators. No individuals in view.

Both quantifier and algebraic generalism are *holistic*.[17] To see this, consider a situation the fundamental nature of which is exhaustively characterized, according to the individualist, by the following facts:

$$a \text{ is } F$$
$$b \text{ is } G$$
$$a \text{ bears } R \text{ to } b$$
$$a \neq b$$

How would the quantifier generalist characterise the fundamental facts of this situation? Not as

$$(\exists x) \, x \text{ is } F$$
$$(\exists x) \, x \text{ is } G$$
$$(\exists x)(\exists y) \, x \text{ bears } R \text{ to } y$$
$$(\exists x)(\exists y) \, x \neq y$$

for this leaves open whether the thing that is F is the same as the thing that is G, and whether it is the same as the thing that bears R to something, and so on. The trouble is that the variables in this list are not 'coordinated'. To coordinate them, the quantifier generalist must express the fundamental nature of the situation all at once, as

($) $(\exists x)(\exists y)(x \text{ is } F \ \& \ y \text{ is } G \ \& \ x \neq y \ \& \ x \text{ bears } R \text{ to } y)$

This is not to deny that the four 'smaller' existentially quantified facts listed above obtain in the situation. They do. It is just to say that they are not fundamental: they hold in virtue of ($).

Precisely the same goes for algebraic generalism too—which should not be surprising, given that the operations of algebraic generalism are designed to mimic first-order logic. Thus, to characterize the situation just discussed, the algebraic generalist will construct a complex state of affairs that characterizes the situation as a whole, and the fundamental fact (according to her) will be that that state of affairs obtains.

Thus, while the individualist thinks that the world at its most fundamental level decomposes into a number of distinct atomic facts, both generalists disagree: for them, the world is at rock bottom a unified whole. That is the respect in which both generalist views are holistic.

4. Plural Grounding

So much for the first question, concerning what kinds of qualitative facts are fundamental. The second question remains: Are they sufficient to ground the individualistic facts?

If not, the qualitativist must embrace an error theory and say that there are no individualistic facts and (therefore) no individuals such as apples, alligators, or atoms. On this view, what we discovered to be the fundamental facts of the world are not sufficient to ground this aspect of the manifest image.[18]

But one might argue that an error theory about the existence of individuals is intolerable (I have some sympathy with this line of thought). If so, the qualitativist must show that individualistic facts *are* explicable in terms of the qualitative basis after all. And this is surprisingly hard to do.

The problem arises when one attends to two constraints governing ground, namely that a grounding explanation must both *necessitate* and be *explanatorily relevant* to what it grounds. Consider the fact that a particular apple A exists. By Necessitation—the principle introduced in section 1—whatever grounds its existence must necessitate its existence. But what qualitative facts could necessitate this? Not the fact that some apple or other exists, since this does not necessitate A's existence: another apple could exist without A existing. Nor the fact that some apple has various qualities and exists in certain qualitatively specified local conditions—e.g. is red, is near a silver laptop, etc.— since that does not necessitate A's existence either (there is a possible world in which there are qualitatively identical local conditions in Moscow even though A does not exist). The only qualitative fact that might necessitate A's existence is the qualitative state of a very large region of spacetime—perhaps the state of the entire cosmos. But the problem is that such a state will include qualitative information that is *irrelevant* to an explanation of A's existence, e.g. information about the state of Alpha Centauri. If I asked you to explain why (in the grounding sense) A exists, and you started talking about events in Alpha Centauri, I would accuse you of wandering off topic: intuitively, such events are *explanatorily irrelevant* to why A exists. This idea that events in Alpha Centauri are irrelevant is not something we can give up just because we are generalists. Rather (the argument is) this idea is central to our understanding of what the apple A is: if qualitativism cannot accommodate it, then qualitativism cannot accommodate the apple.

This is not to say that *no* qualitative facts are relevant to an explanation of A's existence. The qualitative state of a small region around the cup might be relevant. But (as we saw) that does not necessitate its existence. So the argument is this. When it comes to finding a qualitative ground for a given individualistic fact, the two constraints that a ground must both *necessitate* and be *explanatorily relevant* cannot be jointly met: either the putative ground necessitates but is irrelevant, or it is relevant but does not necessitate.[19]

The solution, I think, is to relax the logical form that grounding explanations can take. The above argument assumes that the qualitativist must find a qualitative ground for each individualistic fact in turn. But what if grounding explanations can be non-distributively plural, where this means that a plurality of facts taken together, the Xs, are grounded in some others, even though no one of the Xs has a ground on its own? If so, the qualitativist can say that the individualistic facts are *plurally* grounded in the qualitative facts in this non-distributive sense: *they*, the individualist facts taken together, *are* grounded in qualitative facts, even though no individualistic fact taken on its own has a qualitative ground. This solution concedes the argument (above) that there is no qualitative explanation of why the apple A exists, and yet agrees with the qualitativist that the world is fundamentally qualitative.

This solution arguably satisfies the two constraints that grounds both necessitate and are relevant. For the question is whether all the qualitative facts (taken together) necessitate and are relevant to all the individualistic facts (taken together). And the answer in both cases is plausibly 'Yes'.

If this solution is right, it might explain why individualism is often considered the more natural view. For the solution implies that if one looks at an individualistic fact on its own, one will not find a qualitative ground for it; and it is easy to infer from this to the conclusion that qualitativism is false. The inference is invalid if ground is non-distributively plural, but the mistake is understandable.

There is much more to say about how plural explanations work and whether this specific explanatory proposal is plausible. But I cannot discuss it all here; for now, I can only suggest that this idea of plural grounding is a promising option for the qualitativist.[20]

5. Applications

So far, I have motivated qualitativism and outlined some qualitativist views about what the fundamental facts are like, including the one I prefer, algebraic generalism. I also outlined how individualistic facts might be grounded in a qualitative basis.

Suppose you are convinced. What of it? Are there any applications, any issues on which generalism might shed light?

There are. Here I will outline two from the philosophy of physics. The first concerns the metaphysics of spacetime. Many contemporary philosophers of physics are attracted by substantivalism, the view that spacetime exists independently of matter. But substantivalism faces the notorious 'problem of shifts': it appears to imply that uniformly shifting the matter around, while preserving the relations between bits of matter, yields a genuinely distinct possible world (after all, each bit of matter would be situated in a *different* region of spacetime).

Precisely what these shifts are, and why they are problematic, varies across physical theories. With classical theories, the shifts are uniform translations in space—e.g. shifting all matter over 3 feet to the right—and the putative problem is that the differences between worlds related by such a shift are undetectable and physically redundant (see section 2).[21] In General Relativity, the shifts are diffeomorphisms, and the putative problem is that they imply that General Relativity is indeterministic. This is the famous 'Hole Argument'.[22]

In both cases, the difference between worlds related by the shift is merely haecceitistic: the two worlds are qualitatively alike. For example, worlds related by a uniform translation in space differ only with respect to which particular region of space each bit of matter is located at. So, if anti-haecceitism is true, the shift arguments fail. But in section 1 we saw that qualitativism implies anti-haecceitism. Thus, if a substantivalist were also a qualitativist, neither shift argument would get off the ground!

To be clear, the idea of responding to these shift arguments by endorsing *anti-haecceitism* is not new: Butterfield (1988), Maidens (1992), Brighouse (1994), Hoefer (1996), Pooley (2006 and manuscript), and Caulton and Butterfield (2012) all respond this way. Some endorse a counterpart theoretic view of *de re* modality that is thought to imply anti-haecceitism; others take the anti-haecceitism to follow from some other modal axiom. But they all appear to be working with an individualistic conception of spacetime. So their anti-haecceitism is an *addition* to their view of spacetime, in the sense that their individualistic view of spacetime does not *by itself* imply anti-haecceitism. As it were, their anti-haecceitism is an extra thesis that must be put in 'by hand'.

This should strike us as odd. For when substantivalists are faced with other possibilities that look problematic—e.g. the boosts discussed in section 2—the orthodox response is *not* just to tack on an additional modal thesis that implies that boosts are impossible. Rather, it is to endorse a view of the fundamental nature of spacetime that *by itself* yields the result that boosts are impossible.[23] Endorsing qualitativism about spacetime is the analogous move in the case of shifts, for this is a view about the fundamental nature of spacetime that yields *by itself* the result that shifts are impossible, without the need for an additional modal thesis.

So that is one application of qualitativism: it is the natural substantivalist response to the problem of shifts, more natural than other responses that build in the anti-haecceitism 'by hand'.[24]

Admittedly, if the *only* qualitativist view on offer were the traditional bundle theory, this would all be moot. For it is difficult to see how the traditional bundle theory could be true of points of spacetime. At least in classical (flat) spacetimes, the kinds of properties that could be used to bundle a spacetime point—e.g. *being point-sized*, *being a spacetime region*—hold of *all* spacetime points, so the bundle theorist will identify all spacetime points with the very same set and say that there is only one spacetime point! This is clearly intolerable.[25]

But as we have seen, the traditional bundle theory is not the only qualitativist view on offer: there is also generalism of one kind or another. And there are no obvious obstacles in the way of the substantivalist endorsing generalism. So my advice to the substantivalist is: endorse generalism instead.

A second issue illuminated by generalism is this. Many contemporary philosophers of physics are attracted by what they call 'structural realism'. They are moved to this view by a number of considerations, including the Hole Argument (mentioned above), entangled quantum particles, and constancy across theory change, among other things.[26]

But what exactly is structural realism? Its adherents are notoriously unclear. Ladyman and Ross (2007) offer the following:

> There are objects in our metaphysics, but they have been purged of their intrinsic natures, identity, and individuality, and they are not metaphysically fundamental.
>
> (p. 131)

But this talk of 'identity' and 'individuality' is obscure in the extreme—indeed it is emblematic of the kind of metaphysics they purport to disdain! Moreover, the description is only negative, telling us what objects are *not*, but not what they *are*. And when something positive is said, it is hardly enlightening. Thus they say

> There are no things. Structure is all there is.
>
> (p. 130)

But what exactly is structure? We are not told. As a result, it is easy to doubt whether there is a coherent view lying behind the quotes.[27]

Generalism is a view very much in the ballpark of what these quotes gesture at. If so, it serves as a 'proof by construction' that there are coherent views corresponding to the quotes. Thus, generalism is a natural resource for structural realists keen on developing their views.

6. Conclusion

The world is a purely qualitative mosaic. That is the slogan, and I believe it corresponds to something true.

It is less clear which precise qualitativist theory it corresponds to, but my best guess is this. At rock bottom, there is the World Fact of the algebraic generalist: it details how various qualities are stitched together, and constitutes an entire specification of the state of the world all at once. Individualistic facts—that this electron is charged, that this quark has a certain spin—*plurally* hold in virtue of that World Fact: *they*, the individualistic facts taken together, hold in virtue of the World Fact, even though no individualistic fact taken on its own holds in virtue of anything. Quantified facts then hold in virtue of their instances (*contra* the quantified generalist) just as we always thought.

The resulting view is 'structuralist' or 'holistic' in two respects. First, one can state something fundamental only by characterizing the fundamental nature of the world as a whole. And second, the derivative individualistic facts then flow from that fundamental fact only as a group, not one by one. So there is no making sense of *either* the fundamental *or* the derivative without making sense of everything at once.

So, this is what might be called a 'many-from-one' metaphysics, on which many elements (the individualistic facts) flow together from one source (the World Fact). I am not aware of other many-from-one views in recent metaphysics, but Spinoza arguably endorsed one when he argued that the finite modes flow together, but not individually, from the essence of God.[28] If I am right, we have good reason to revisit many-from-one views today.[29]

Notes

1. This claim—that his view is widely shared—is hard to substantiate without lengthy exegetical discussion. But it will become apparent once we see what is involved in thinking that the world is constituted by purely qualitative facts.
2. To be clear on scope, F is individualistic iff there is an x (or there are some Xs) such that whether F obtains depends on how things stand with x (or with the Xs).
3. This is just a rough characterization of the distinction between qualitative and individualistic facts, not a reductive definition. Still, the distinction is clear enough to work with.
4. A different approach uses the notion of *structure* (Sider 2011), saying that only qualitative notions are structural. Yet another uses the notion of *dependence* (Fine 1995; Koslicki 2013), saying that individuals depend on qualities. And yet another uses the notion of *truth-making* (Armstrong 2004; Cameron 2010), saying that all truths are made true by some qualitative fact. And there are other approaches too; see Bennett (forthcoming).
5. This formulation of the issue slurs over a number of difficulties. For one, suppose there is an infinite descending chain of ground that alternates between individualistic and qualitative facts. Then both views *as defined* in the text are true, yet the situation violates the intuitive picture behind both. But fixing these subtleties would distract from the core idea, which I trust is clear enough.
6. This thesis can be precisified in a number of ways, some with modal operators and others with quantification over worlds. These details will not matter here.
7. This principle is widely endorsed by grounding theorists. See in particular Fine (2012), Rosen (2010), and Trogdon (2013b). For dissent, see Schaffer (2010) and Leuenberger (2014).

8. These quotations are, respectively, from Locke (1977, II xxiii 2); Russell (1948a); and Russell (1948b).

9. As I argue in Dasgupta (2016), this is not quite true. But it is close enough to the truth for our purposes here.

10. Adams (1979) discusses this kind of objection at length.

11. See Hacking (1975) and O'Leary-Hawthorne (1995).

12. Paul (2014) also explores various qualitativist views that purport to make perfect sense of symmetric situations. Unfortunately, there is no room to discuss how our views relate here.

13. The claim that this is analytic does not imply the implausible claim that anyone possessing the concept 'something' be familiar with the recent literature on grounding explanations. For that literature aims to describe a concept we already had and used, not introduce a new one.

14. I mentioned this consideration against quantifier generalism in Dasgupta (2009) and (2011). Later I became less confident in it, though Russell's work has convinced me that there might be something to it after all. Clearly, there is more work to do on this issue.

15. See Quine (1976) and Kuhn (1983) for a more detailed treatment of these operations. Note that here I am introducing the properties of the algebraic generalist by saying how we ordinarily talk about them. One might complain that the properties of the algebraic generalist cannot be *the same* as the ones we *ordinarily* talk about, since the latter are essentially had by individuals. But if so, the proper thing to say is that the algebraic generalist is introducing surrogate properties to stand in for the ones of ordinary discourse. I have nothing against this alternative way of talking. Thanks to Michaela McSweeney for a discussion of this point.

16. See Dasgupta (2009) for a more detailed discussion of what this means and why it is so.

17. In Dasgupta (2009), I discuss this aspect of the views in more detail.

18. This is analogous to Mackie's (1977) view of morals, and Boghossian and Velleman's (1989) view of color. In each case, the idea is that what we have (supposedly) discovered to be the fundamental facts—e.g. physical facts concerning the distribution of physical magnitudes—are not sufficient to account for morals or color, respectively.

19. I develop this argument in more detail in Dasgupta (2014).

20. See Dasgupta (2014) for a more thorough development and defense of this idea.

21. For further discussion, see Sklar (1974: ch 3) and Maudlin (1993).

22. See Earman and Norton (1987).

23. I am thinking of the orthodox move of endorsing a Galilean (sometimes called Neo-Newtonian) view of the structure of spacetime.

24. This is the moral of Dasgupta (2011), where I expand on these points.

25. The issue is less clear in curved spacetimes, since the curvature at each point might be used to distinguish them. But I leave this for others to pursue. Strikingly, when working in a classical setting, O'Leary-Hawthorne and Cover (1998) endorse this position that the bundle theory is true of points of substantival spacetime, and they embrace the result that there is only one point! According to them, the One Point stands in many distance relations to itself: it is 1 ft from itself, 2 ft from itself, and so on. They recognize that the view faces difficulties and say that 'further development of this metaphysic must be postponed to another occasion' (p. 212). But they appear not to have appreciated the severity of its difficulties. The whole point of substantivalism is to ground facts about distances between material bodies in terms of their locations in spacetime: considerations such as the bucket argument are taken by substantivalists to show that distances between material bodies cannot be fundamental. But on O'Leary-Hawthorne and Cover's view, all material bodies are located at the same point. If that point is both 1 ft from itself and 2 ft from itself, how far apart are the material bodies? Their locations in substantival space do not answer the question. So their distances must be taken as an extra, fundamental, fact. Which is to say that, on their view, distances between

material bodies are fundamental after all. Which is to say that calling their view "substantivalist" is a sham.
26. See Ladyman and Ross (2007), and references therein.
27. I have heard this doubt regularly in conversation. Admittedly, I am choosing quotes congenial to my point, but I believe the quotes are representative enough for the point being made.
28. See Garrett (1991) for a defense of this reading of Spinoza.
29. Many thanks to Robbie Hirsch, Michaela McSweeney, and John Morrison. Their insightful (and timely) feedback was invaluable.

References

Adams, R. 1979. "Primitive Thisness and Primitive Identity". *The Journal of Philosophy* 76 (1): 5–26.
Armstrong, D. 2004. *Truth and Truthmakers*. Cambridge: Cambridge University Press.
Baker, D. 2010. "Symmetry and the Metaphysics of Physics". *Philosophy Compass* 5 (12): 1157–1166.
Bennett, K. Forthcoming. *Making Things Up*. Oxford: Oxford University Press.
Boghossian, P. and D. Velleman. 1989. "Colour as a Secondary Quality". *Mind* 98: 81–103.
Brighouse, C. 1994. "Spacetime and Holes". *PSA: Proceedings of the Biennial Meeting of the Philosophy of Science Association* 1: 117–125.
Butterfield, J. 1988. "Albert Einstein Meets David Lewis". *PSA: The Proceedings of the Biennial Meeting of the Philosophy of Science Association* 2: 65–81.
Cameron, R. 2010. "How to Have a Radically Minimal Ontology". *Philosophical Studies* 151: 249–264.
Caulton, A. and J. Butterfield. 2012. "Symmetries and Paraparticles as a Motivation for Structuralism". *British Journal for the Philosophy of Science* 63 (2): 233–285.
Dasgupta, S. 2009. "Individuals: An Essay in Revisionary Metaphysics". *Philosophical Studies* 145 (1): 35–67.
———. 2011. "The Bare Necessities". *Philosophical Perspectives* 25 (1): 115–160.
———. 2014. "On the Plurality of Grounds". *Philosophers' Imprint* 14: 1–28.
———. 2016. "Symmetry as an Epistemic Notion (Twice Over)". *The British Journal for the Philosophy of Science* 67: 837–878.
Earman, J. and J. Norton. 1987. "What Price Substantivalism? The Hole Story". *The British Journal for the Philosophy of Science* 38: 515–525.
Fine, K. 1995. "Ontological Dependence". *Proceedings of the Aristotelian Society* 95: 269–290.
———. 2001. "The Question of Realism". *Philosophers' Imprint* 1 (2): 1–30.
———. 2012. "Guide to Ground". In F. Correia and B. Schneider (eds.), *Metaphysical Grounding: Understanding the Structure of Reality*, 37–80. Cambridge: Cambridge University Press.
Garrett, D. 1991. 'Spinoza's Necessitarianism'. In Y. Yovel (ed.), *God and Nature: Spinoza's Metaphysics*, 191–218.
Hacking, I. 1975. "The Identity of Indiscernibles". *Journal of Philosophy* 72 (9): 249–256.
Hoefer, C. 1996. "The Metaphysics of Space-Time Substantivalism". *The Journal of Philosophy* 93 (1): 5–27.
Koslicki, K. 2013. "Ontological Dependence: An Opinionated Survey". In B. Schneider, M. Hoeltje, and A. Steinberg (eds.), *Varieties of Dependence: Ontological Dependence, Grounding, Supervenience, Response Dependence (Basic Philosophical Concepts)*, 31–64. Munich: Philosophia Verlag.
Kuhn, S. (1983). An Axiomatization of Predicate Functor Logic. Notre Dame Journal of Formal Logic 24(2): 233–241.
Ladyman, J. and D. Ross. 2007. *Every Thing Must Go: Metaphysics Naturalized*. Oxford: Oxford University Press.
Leuenberger, S. 2014. "Grounding and Necessity". *Inquiry* 57 (2): 151–174.
Lewis, D. 1986. *On the Plurality of Worlds*. Oxford: Blackwell.

Locke, J. 1977. *An Essay Concerning Human Understanding*. Ed. R. Woolhouse. London: Penguin Books.

Mackie, J.L. 1977. *Ethics: Inventing Right and Wrong*. London: Penguin Books.

Maidens, A. 1992. "Review of John Earman's World Enough and Space-Time". *The British Journal for the Philosophy of Science* 43 (1): 129–136.

Maudlin, T. 1993. "Buckets of Water and Waves of Space: Why Spacetime Is Probably a Substance". *Philosophy of Science* 60 (2): 183–203.

O'Leary-Hawthorne, J. 1995. "The Bundle Theory of Substance and the Identity of Indiscernibles". *Analysis* 55: 191–196.

O'Leary-Hawthorne, J. and J.A. Cover. 1998. "A World of Universals". *Philosophical Studies* 91: 205–219.

Paul, L.A. 2012. "Building the World from Its Fundamental Constituents". *Philosophical Studies* 158 (2): 221–256.

———. Forthcoming. "A One Category Ontology". In J. A. Keller (ed.), *Being, Freedom, and Method: Themes from van Inwagen*. Oxford: Oxford University Press.

Pooley, O. 2006. "Points, Particles, and Structural Realism". In D. Rickles, S. French, and J. Saatsi (eds.), *The Structural Foundations of Quantum Gravity*, 83–120. Oxford: Oxford University Press.

———. Manuscript. *Substantivalism and Haecceitism*.

Quine, W. V. (1976). Algebraic Logic and Predicate Functors. In his "The Ways of Paradox and Other Essays" (2nd ed., pp. 283–307). Cambridge MA: Harvard University Press.

Rosen, G. 2010. "Metaphysical Dependence: Grounding and Reduction". In B. Hale and A. Hoffmann (eds.), *Modality: Metaphysics, Logic, and Epistemology*, 109–136. Oxford: Oxford University Press.

Russell, B. 1948a. *Human Knowledge: Its Scope and Limits*. New York: Simon and Schuster.

Russell, B. 1948b. *An Inquiry into Meaning and Truth*. London: Allen and Unwin.

Russell, J. Manuscript. "Quality and Quantifiers".

Schaffer, J. 2009. "On What Grounds What". In D. Manley, D. Chalmers, and R. Wasserman (eds.), *Metametaphysics*, 347–383. Oxford: Oxford University Press.

———. 2010. "The Least Discerning and Most Promiscuous Truth-Maker". *The Philosophical Quarterly* 60: 307–324.

Sider, T. 2011. *Writing the Book of the World*. Oxford: Oxford University Press.

Sklar, L. 1974. *Space, Time, and Spacetime*. Berkeley, CA: University of California Press.

Trogdon, K. 2013a. "Grounding: Necessary or Contingent?" *Pacific Philosophical Quarterly* 94 (4): 465–485.

———. 2013b. "An Introduction to Grounding". In M. Hoeltje, B. Schnieder, and A. Steinberg (eds.), *Varieties of Dependence: Ontological Dependence, Grounding, Supervenience, Response Dependence (Basic Philosophical Concepts)*, 97–122. Munich: Philosophia Verlag.

CHAPTER 2

Can We Do Without Fundamental Individuals? No*

JASON TURNER

According to *qualitativism*, individuals aren't 'primitive', or fundamental; all fundamental facts are purely qualitative. Some reasons to believe it are narrowly scientific, stemming from (for instance) concerns about quantum probabilities (cf. French and Krause 2006: chs. 3–4). Others may be purely *a priori*, stemming from Berkelean qualms about the very idea of an individual abstracted from its properties and relations. But I will follow Dasgupta by focusing on a *broad* scientific argument for qualitativism. It goes like this: Since Newton on, science has only cared about the natural qualities individuals have, and not which individuals have them. Individuals are thus explanatorily idle, not earning their theoretical keep. If we can help it, we shouldn't think idlers—including individuals —are fundamental.

Can we help it? I'm not yet convinced. I worry that theories which avoid fundamental individuals fall prey to the problems that beset fundamental individuals in the first place. My goal here is to sketch my worries.

1. The Idler Argument

Dasgupta's broadly scientific argument is a theory choice argument. We generally should prefer simpler, elegant theories to complex or baroque ones. If two theories explain the data equally well but one is more 'theoretically virtuous' than another—is more simple, elegant, etc., than the other—we ought to accept the more virtuous one.

An *explanatory idler* is a feature of a theory that does no explanatory work. For instance, in Newtonian mechanics, absolute velocity was an explanatory idler: it played no role in explaining any phenomenon. Subsequent physicists preferred the 'neo-Newtonian' theory gotten by removing absolute velocity. That's because idlers are a theoretical vice. We ought to prefer theories without idlers to those with them.[1]

Principles of theory choice are *ceteris paribus*. If one theory has a virtue another lacks and *all else is equal*, prefer the theory with the extra virtue. All else is equal between Newtonian and neo-Newtonian physics, so we prefer the latter. But matters are more complex when not all else is equal. If two otherwise equally good theories each has a virtue the other lacks, we'll have to do some complex balancing up.

Dasgupta's argument only relies on a weak principle of theory choice which says we should prefer *fundamental* theories without idlers to those with them.[2]

The argument runs:

The Idler Argument

    (I.i)   If I is a fundamental theory that posits individuals, then it has a counterpart theory Q which does not posit individuals.

    (I.ii) Individuals are explanatory idlers.

    (I.iii) If all else is equal, we ought to prefer fundamental theories that do not posit explanatory idlers over ones that do.

    (I.iv) All else is equal with I and Q.

    (I.v) So we ought to prefer I to Q.

If the argument is good, then every fundamental individualistic theory I is bested by an individual-free theory Q, so we ought not accept any fundamental individualistic theory.

Arguments are no more compelling than their premises. Start with premise (I.ii). Dasgupta (2009), extrapolating from physics, identifies two criteria he thinks jointly sufficient for idleness. One is empirical undetectability: no possible experiment distinguishes systems where the idlers are different. The second is physical redundancy: the physics pays no attention to the idlers themselves. Premise (I.ii) is justified because individuals meet both criteria. No experiment can tell whether a system has an individual a or a perfect qualitative duplicate b, and a system's evolution doesn't depend on which individuals have which physical properties.

Next, premise (I.i). To defend it, we need a recipe for trading any individualist theory for an individual-free counterpart. I'll look at three attempts below. The most straightforward strategy (§2) faces a worry Dasgupta raises for it (this volume, p. 13). I'll argue the other strategies (§§3–4) either fall to the same worry or are threatened by the Idler Argument.

2. Quantifier Generalism

A theory is individualist if it says there are fundamental 'individual facts'. And a fact is an 'individual fact' if it can be expressed by a sentence that uses an individual's name—such as '*Fa*' or '*Pa* & *Qa*', where '*a*' names an individual.[3] To avoid individualism, we might insist that all fundamental facts are quantificational, expressed by sentences such as '∃*xFx*' or '∀*y*(*Py* & *Qy*)'. Then we trade *I* for *Q* by trading fundamental individual facts for their existential counterparts.[4] Call the theory *Q* generated this way *I*'s *existential closure*. *Quantifier generalism* holds that the fundamental theory is the existential closure of some true-but-not-fundamental theory.

Dasgupta worries that quantifier generalism can't be right. Here's why. It's natural to think that existential quantifications are grounded in their instances: the truth of 'Something is *F*' is grounded in an *F* individual (cf. e.g. Rosen 2010: 117). More precisely (and to avoid scope ambiguities):

∃-**Ground:** If ∃*xFx*, then for some *y*, the fact that ∃*xFx* is grounded in the fact that *Fy*.

But fundamental facts should be ungrounded—that's what it *is* to be fundamental.[5] This tells us:

Fund-Ground: For all *y* and *P*, if the fact that *P* is grounded in the fact that *Fy*, then it is not fundamental that *P*.

But now we can give

The Grounding Argument

(G.i) If ∃*xFx*, then for some *y*, the fact that ∃*xFx* is grounded in the fact that *Fy*.
∃-Ground

(G.ii) If for some *y*, the fact that ∃*xFx* is grounded in the fact that *Fy*, then it is not fundamental that ∃*xFx*.
Fund-Ground

(G.iii) So if ∃*xFx*, it is not fundamental that ∃*xFx*. from (G.i), (G.ii)

This is a perfectly general argument that existential quantifications can't be fundamental truths. Since quantifier generalism says that some existential quantifications *are* fundamental truths, this argument rules it out.

3. Algebraic Generalism

So fundamental facts can't be quantificational. They can have the form of '*Fa*', '*Pb* & *Qb*', or similar, so long as '*a*', '*b*', and so on aren't names for individuals.

Algebraic generalism is a theory where fundamental facts have these forms, but the names are names for *properties and relations*. We will treat properties as one-placed relations: the difference between a property and a dyadic relation is the same as that between a dyadic relation and a triadic relation. There are also *zero-place* relations—abstract entities that differ from properties just as properties differ from dyadic relations.

Intuitively, *n*-adic relations are instantiated by *n* things. But zero-place relations can be instantiated by *zero* things. We can think of zero-place relations as analogous to propositions or abstract states-of-affairs and, when one is instantiated, we say that it *obtains*. The algebraic generalist thinks that, in the first instance, fundamental facts are of the form

(1) Obtains(p),

where p is a zero-place relation.

The algebraic generalist thinks that relations are algebraically related to each other. For instance, each relation has a negation, and any two relations have a conjunction. We use '¬' and '∧' for them. If 'p' and 'q' are names for relations, then '¬p' and '$p \land q$' are names for p's negation and its conjunction with q, respectively.

There are some less familiar algebraic relations, too. For instance, relations have 'inversions'. If 'r' names the *attracting* relation, then '$\sigma(r)$' names its inversion, the *being attracted by* relation.[6] More importantly, there is the *cropping* relation. If r is an n-placed relation, $c(r)$ is a relation with one less place.[7]

What is cropping? At a first pass, we can think of it as existential quantification. If r is the *attracting* relation, we can think of $c(r)$ as the property of *attracting something*. Likewise, if n is the *negative charge* property, we can think of $c(n)$ as the zero-place relation (or state of affairs) of *something being negatively charged*.

The algebraic generalist doesn't want us to take that gloss too literally. He says our licence to think of c as existential quantification does *not* come from $c(p)$ being fundamentally 'about' individuals having p. The explanation goes the other way 'round. We can think of c as existential quantification thanks to how it relates to the non-fundamental. Suppose, for instance, that

(2) $\exists x(Px \,\&\, Qx)$

is true. According to the algebraic generalist, its truth is ultimately grounded in

(3) Obtains($c(p \land q)$).

In general, truths expressed with an existential quantifier will be grounded in zero-placed relations that have 'c's more-or-less where the original truth had existential quantifiers.[8]

The good news for algebraic generalism is that every first-order sentence can be 'translated' into a corresponding zero-placed relation. So each individualist theory I has an algebraic generalist counterpart Q, vindicating premise (I.i).

But I worry that algebraic generalism fails to play nicely with the Idler Argument in other ways. The rest of this section will explain why.

3.1. Logical Double-Counting

(2) entails

(4) $\exists x Px$.

As a result, (3) should entail

(5) Obtains($c(p)$).

More generally, logical relations between quantified claims correspond to logical relations between zero-placed properties. How should the functorese generalist deal with this?

The most natural suggestion involves *entailments* between properties. Intuitively, anything that has the conjunctive property $p \wedge q$ ought to have both p and q. So $p \wedge q$ ought to entail p, and it ought to entail q. And this ought to be perfectly general: conjunctive relations should entail their conuncts. If we write entailment as '$\Rightarrow$', we can express this as

(6) $\forall x \forall y (x \wedge y \Rightarrow x)$.

Inferences using existential quantifiers will correspond to entailments involving c. These entailments ought to make c behave in existential-quantifier-like ways. The validity of existential generalization will correspond to

(7) $\forall x (x \Rightarrow c(x))$.

Since existential instantiation is a complicated rule, c's corresponding entailments will be complicated too. But at a very rough first pass we could use

(8) $\forall xy(\text{If } x \Rightarrow y, \text{ then } c(x) \Rightarrow y)$.[9]

If we also have a rule that says that entailment is transitive,

(9) $\forall x \forall y \forall z(\text{If } x \Rightarrow y \, \& \, y \Rightarrow z \text{ then } x \Rightarrow z)$,

we can use (6)–(9) to conclude

(10) $c(p \, \& \, q) \Rightarrow c(p)$.[10]

If we also have a principle which tells us that, if one property entails another and the first obtains, the second also obtains, we can get from (3) to (5).

Everything that has an explanation has a *fundamental* explanation. If (6)–(9) are the fundamental explanation for the entailment between (2) and (4), they had better be fundamental themselves. In this case, some fundamental facts are logically complex.[11]

This means fundamental facts will make use of two kinds of logical resources. One kind shows up in the names for the relations: ¬, ∧, and so on. The other kind is used to conjoin or negate sentences. And we will have to double up on logical axioms, too. For instance, we'll have quality-level conjunction elimination, (6), as well as a sentence-level one,

(11) If *P* & *Q*, then *P*.

As a result, our theory kills one bird with two stones. We generally want our theories to avoid this kind of excess, dealing with similar phenomena in one way rather than many. When all else is equal, we ought to prefer theories that have just one kind of conjunction, and one fundamental principle to handle it, rather than two.

Of course, when algebraic generalism is pitted against an individualist theory, the qualitativist will say that not all else is equal. The individualist has idlers that the algebraic generalist lacks. Avoiding those idlers may be worth the price of some logical double-counting.

Fair enough. But sauce for the goose is sauce for the gander, as they say: the individualist may well think that it's worth paying the cost of idlers to avoid this sort of logical duplication. This suggests that, when Q is the algebraic generalist's counterpart of the individualist theory I, not all else is equal between them. Premise (I.iv) of the Idler Argument does not go through, and reasonable people can prefer individualism's idlers over algebraic generalism's excess logical structure.

3.2. The Idlers' Revenge

As I wrote it, the Idler Argument is invalid. It needs an extra premise:

(I.ii$\frac{1}{2}$) If Q does not posit individuals, it does not posit explanatory idlers.

If Q is as lousy with explanatory idlers as I is, then its lack of individuals is no reason to favour it. But we might worry that the relations *themselves* are explanatory idlers. In that case, (I.ii$\frac{1}{2}$) is false and the argument doesn't go through.

Why think they're explanatory idlers? For one thing, they're *empirically undetectable*.[12] Empirical undetectability in individuals means that, if God replaced one individual for another that is intrinsically just like it, no experiment could detect the difference. If we had a long complex sentence S that completely described an individual x, and if God traded x for an individual y that was equally well described by S, we couldn't tell the difference.

Let q be a relation and S a long sentence that completely describes it. Then S must describe, in part, how q interacts with experimental equipment and the like. So if God replaced q for a relation p that was equally well described by S, we couldn't tell the difference. Any experiment we might perform would give us the same results with q swapped for p.

If relations are also physically redundant, they will meet Dasgupta's two criteria for idleness. Here's a quick argument that they are. To fix ideas, suppose that there is just one law of physics, which says that all Fs are Gs:

(12) $\forall x(Fx \rightarrow Gx)$.

According to algebraic generalism, this is grounded in the obtaining of a certain zero-place relation:

(13) $\text{Obtains}(\neg c \neg (f \wedge \neg g))$.

But since f and g are empirically undetectable, whatever evidence supports it equally well supports

(14) $\exists x \exists y(\text{Obtains}(\neg c \neg (x \wedge \neg y)))$.

So (14) has as much claim to lawhood as (12) has. In that case, the individual properties f and g are themselves physically redundant: the laws only care that *some* relations are distributed in a certain way, not that f and g are. And this argument is perfectly general. If there are many and complex laws, we replace (12) With their conjunction and reason the same way

If this argument goes through, then relations are idlers, and algebraic generalism is no better off than individualism on that front. But the argument can be resisted. One natural line of resistance insists that the laws *aren't* of (14)'s form. The laws of physics are what physicists investigate, and physicists *do* care about precisely which properties figure in the laws. They would consider set-ups where not all Fs are Gs as physically different, even if (say) all Ps were Qs. So relations are not physically redundant.

Rather than worrying about the sociology of physics, I'll grant the point: the algebraic generalist's relations are not physically redundant. Still, there is reason to think that they are explanatorily idle. In physics, explanations come by combining laws with initial conditions. For instance, we might explain why x is G by combining the initial condition of its being F with the law (12). But we could just as well explain it by combining the initial condition of x and y being an individual and a property where (i) x has y and (ii) y satisfies (14) along with g. The second sort of explanation seems just as good as the first. But the second sort doesn't care *which* relation is involved in satisfying (14).[13]

Granted, that's not how *physicists* do it. They give explanations of the first sort. But so what? We can imagine a possible community of scientists that explain things in the second way, and they don't seem to be doing anything wrong. Conversely, we can imagine a possible community of scientists who insist on explanations where individuals' identities are listed in the initial conditions. That community will consider situations that swap an individual for a physical duplicate to be physically distinct. But that doesn't mean that the individuals aren't explanatorily redundant. Unless we have special reason to think that our scientists are better than their merely possible counterparts in drawing the explanatory lines exactly where they belong there is no straightforward argument from actual scientific practice against relations' idleness.

4. Functorese Generalism

Algebraic generalism is *platonistic*, grounding 'Something is negatively charged' in facts about the property *negative charge*. Nominalists insist that there are no properties or relations and so already won't like algebraic generalism. But they can endorse a nominalized variant.

Nominalists generally trade properties and relations for coherent uses of predicates. They reject *negative charge* as an entity while still granting that some things are negatively charged. The nominalized variant of algebraic generalism trades relations for predicates and trades the algebraic '$\wedge$', '$\neg$', 'c', etc. for *predicate functors*—devices that turn less complex predicates into more complex ones. For instance, if 'P' and 'Q' are simple predicates, then '$P \wedge Q$' is a complex one that counts as their conjunction.

On this theory, 'c' turns many-placed predicates into predicates with one fewer place. Zero-placed predicates are *sentences*, and can be asserted or denied. Instead of saying that a complex property obtains (as (3) did) we assert the complex sentence

(15) $c(P \wedge Q)$,

and the fact that $c(P \wedge Q)$ is taken to ground (2). Call this view *functorese generalism*.

According to functorese generalism, there *are* no relations, so it avoids the idlers of §3.2. And since sentences are just zero-placed predicates, the logical predicate-forming operators are also sentential operators. So we need only one set of logical terms and one set of axioms governing them, avoiding the duplication problems of §3.1.

Although functorese generalism avoids *those* problems, it faces a variant of an argument I gave against a similar view elsewhere (2011). That argument suggests that the cropping connective c is a disguised existential quantifier. In the present context, the worry is that, as a disguised existential quantifier, functorese generalism faces the same problems that quantifier generalism was supposed to.

First, some background. Let L be a first-order language we use to describe the world in terms of individuals. The quantifiers of L, like those in other standard quantificational languages, do two jobs: variable binding and quantification proper. '$\exists x \ldots$' means 'There is something that is an x such that $\ldots$'.

We can break that meaning into two parts. One part means 'There is something that'. The other means 'is an x such that $\ldots$'. The first part quantifies proper. The second binds variables.

So-called *lambda-abstraction languages* use separate expressions for these two parts. The symbol '$\exists_p$' means 'there is something that' and attaches to many-placed predicates to produce predicates with one place fewer. The symbol 'λ' binds variables to create complex predicates. For instance, '$\lambda x(Fx \ \& \ Gx)$' is a complex predicate meaning 'is both F and G'.

For the first step of the argument, let $L\lambda$ be a lambda-abstraction language with the same predicates as L. It should be clear that, if the fact that $\exists x(Fx \ \& \ Gx)$ is grounded in $Fa \ \& \ Ga$, then so is the fact that $\exists_p\lambda x(Fx\&Gx)$.

Variable binding is a way of making complex predicates from simple ones. Existential truths are grounded in their instances thanks to the quantifiers proper, since the existential quantifier proper is the expression which *says* that there is an individual. The argument's second step says that, as a result, we can replace λ with alternative variable-binding resources without changing what quantifications are grounded in. In particular, we can trade λ for the functorese generalist's functors other than c. If the fact that $\exists_p\lambda x(Fx \ \& \ Gx)$ is grounded in $Fa \ \& \ Ga$, for instance, then so is the fact that $\exists_p(F \wedge G)$. After all, we haven't touched '$\exists_p$', the expression that leads to grounding in individuals.

Let $F_{\exists p}$ be the language we get from $L\lambda$ with these replacements, and let F be the language the functorese generalist uses to express fundamental facts. Notice that they're exactly the same except that the latter replaces '$\exists_p$' with 'c'. If the sentences of $F_{\exists p}$ are grounded in individuals and those of F aren't, it had better be because of a difference in meaning between 'c' and '$\exists P$'.

The argument's last step points out that this conflicts with extremely plausible principles of interpretation. Individualists will assent to sentences of $F_{\exists p}$ exactly when functorese generalists assent to sentences of F just like them but for the replacement of '$\exists_p$' with 'c'. Consider the following very weak principle of interpretation:

(*) If L_1 and L_2 are languages with all terms in common except that L_2 has a term β in place of L_1's term α, and if all shared terms have the same interpretation in both languages, and if speakers of L_1 will assent to a sentence with α when and only when speakers of L_2 will assent to the corresponding sentence with β replaced for α, and vice versa, then α and β have the same interpretation.

According to (*), '$\exists_p$' and 'c' have the same interpretation. But if we trade one symbol for another with the same interpretation, we shouldn't change what grounds what. If sentences of L can't be fundamental thanks to being grounded in individuals, sentences of F can't be, either. If the Grounding Argument rules out quantifier generalism, this extension of it rules out functorese generalism.

5. Conclusion

Is all lost for qualitativism? Not obviously. I've argued against three qualitativist theories. Here are a few ways qualitativists might respond:

- Reject $\exists$-Ground, rehabilitating both quantifier and functorese generalism.
- Give up on the Idler Argument and find a new way to motivate qualitativism that doesn't create problems for algebraic generalism.
- Find some fourth qualitativist theory I haven't discussed.

And there may be more.

While I have some sympathy for the first response, I can't see how the second or third would go. This might just be lack of imagination on my part, of course. But if I have to accept $\exists$-Ground, until I hear more about the second or third option, I'm not yet ready to give up fundamental individuals.

Notes

* Thanks to Jeff Russell, an audience at the Leeds Centre for Metaphysics and Mind, and especially Shamik Dasgupta, for helpful comments and discussion.
1. The argument here follows Dasgupta's 2009, where idlers are called 'danglers'.
2. We can think of 'fundamental theories' as (proposed) lists of fundamental facts.
3. I don't mean anything metaphysically beefy by fact-talk—I suspect what I say about fundamental *facts* can be translated as being about fundamental *truths*. But I won't bother.
4. One method conjoins I's facts into a conjunction C, existentially quantifies into C's name positions (with a different variable for each name), and calls the result Q.

5. At least, that's how Dasgupta is thinking about it. I'm not entirely sold on grounding-driven conceptions of fundamentality, but I'll play along here.
6. There are actually two inversion relations, but they both treat two-placed predicates the same way. There is also a 'padding' relation that effectively 'adds' an argument place. The basic idea can be found in Quine 1960; the details of this particular system are spelled out in Dasgupta 2009, appendix, and elsewhere.
7. When $n \geq 1$.
8. 'More or less' because we have to take the original truth and translate it into one that only uses '∃', '&', and '~' first.
9. Ironing out the roughness requires getting clearer on what it means for relations of different adicies to entail each other. Natural proposals all make (8) unacceptable. A less risky variant restricts (8) to cases where x has a higher adicy than y.
10. By (6), $p \wedge q \Rightarrow p$, and by (7), $p \Rightarrow c(p)$, so by (9) $p \wedge q \Rightarrow c(p)$. We're supposing p and q are both properties, so $p \wedge q$ has a higher adicy than $c(p)$. Thus by (8) (even with the previous note's restrictions), we get $c(p \wedge q) \Rightarrow c(p)$.
11. Note that the Grounding Argument doesn't tell against (6)–(9) being fundamental—it says that *existential* facts can't be fundamental, but doesn't rule out *universal* ones being so.
12. Compare Langton (1998) and Lewis (2009).
13. Well, it cares that g is one of the relations—but that's because g was part of the explanandum. By the same token, the *first* explanation cared that it was x which had G—but again, that was part of the explanadum. Presumably, our explanations of individual-involving explanandum might involve *those* individuals—individuals are 'explanatorily idle' in that they're not needed for any explanations of phenomena when they're not an essential part of the phenomenon in question. By the same token, if we give the second style of explanation, relations aren't needed to explain any phenomena of which they're not an essential part.

References

Dasgupta, S. 2009. "Individuals: An Essay in Revisionary Metaphysics." *Philosophical Studies* 145: 37–67.
French, S. and D. Krause, 2006. *Identity in Physics: A Historical, Philosophical, and Formal Analysis.* Oxford: Oxford University Press.
Langton, R. 1998. *Kantian Humility: Our Ignorance of Things in Themselves.* Oxford: Oxford University Press.
Lewis, D. 2009. "Ramseyan Humility". In D. Braddon-Mitchell and R. Nola (eds.), *Conceptual Analysis and Philosophical Naturalism*, 203–222. Cambridge, MA: MIT Press.
Quine, W. 1960. "Variables Explained Away." *Proceedings of the American Philosophical Society* 104: 343–347. Reprinted in Quine 1966: 227–235.
———. 1966. *Selected Logic Papers.* Cambridge, MA: Harvard University Press.
Rosen, G. 2010. "Metaphysical Dependence: Grounding and Reduction". In B. Hale and A. Hoffman (eds.), *Modality: Metaphysics, Logic, and Epistemology*, 109–135. Oxford: Oxford University Press.
Turner, J. 2011. "Ontological Nihilism". In D.W. Zimmerman and K. Bennett (eds.), *Oxford Studies in Metaphysics*, Volume 6, 1–50. Oxford: Oxford University Press.

Postscript

SHAMIK DASGUPTA AND JASON TURNER

SD: You argued that algebraic generalism faces two problems: logical double-counting and the idler's revenge. You then offered me a chalice in *functorese generalism*, a generalist view which, you say, avoids both problems. But you argued that the chalice is poisoned: it is no better than *quantifier generalism*, a view I am uncertain of.

JT: Right. That's why I'm not yet ready to give up on fundamental individuals.

SD: I think the two problems facing algebraic generalism are not as pressing as you suggest, so I'm happy to concede that your chalice is poisoned. Still, let me raise one worry about your argument against functorese generalism. Could you remind me how it proceeds?

JT: Sure. Assume that *quantifier* generalism is wrong because it violates the principle I called ∃-Ground, which says that existential quantifications are grounded in their instances. If an individual a is F, this principle implies:

$$(1) \quad (\exists x)Fx \text{ because } Fa.$$

The argument's first stage argues from (1) to the truth of its counterpart in the language $F_{\exists p}$ where variable binding is done by operators:

$$(2) \quad \exists_p(F) \text{ because } Fa.$$

The second stage argues that, thanks to the plausible principle of interpretation (*), the symbol 'c' in the language F means the same as '$\exists_p$'. If so, there should be no difference in ground. Thus:

$$(3) \quad c(\text{F}) \text{ because F}a,$$

contra functorese generalism.

SD: Very nice. And your principle (*) is plausible indeed. But it only applies to cases where speakers of the two languages assent to exactly the same sentences, *modulo* substitution of the two terms. If they do, (*) says that the two terms have the same interpretation.

But what if the speakers differ with regards to which sentences they assent to, *precisely on the issue of what grounds what*? Suppose we assent to (1), speakers of $F_{\exists P}$ assent to (2), but speakers of F do *not* assent to (3). Then your principle (*) does not apply and we cannot infer that '$\exists_p$' means the same as 'c'.

Indeed, there might be a divergence in assent *because* of a difference in meaning. Perhaps (1) is analytic of '$(\exists x)$' but (3) is not analytic of 'c'. Thus, while you say 'if the sentences of $F_{\exists P}$ are grounded in individuals and those of F aren't, it had better be because of a difference in meaning between them' (p. 32), the explanation might go the other way: a difference in meaning might explain the difference in ground.

JT: Yes, the functorese generalist might refuse to assert (3), and if so then (*) doesn't apply. But I worry this move cheats.

Imagine a quantifier generalist who, after seeing the Grounding Argument, simply introduces a new expression 'δ'. He insists that it is intersubstitutable *salva veritate* in all 'because'-free contexts, but not in 'because'-using ones. According to him, truths of the form '$\delta x F x$' are not grounded in truths of the forms 'Fa'. This move avoids the Grounding Argument—but smacks of cheating.

SD: Agreed: that certainly is cheating!

JT: The original idea was that (*) told us *why* the δ-move was cheating, and we could use it to expose predicate functorese as similarly cheating—and as hiding the cheat behind irrelevant technicalities about variable binding.

If you're right about (1)–(3), then (*) doesn't quite do the job—for my original argument, and for the $\exists/\delta$ proposal, too, because the δ-user will dissent from

$$(4) \quad (\delta x)\text{F}x \text{ because F}a$$

even while assenting to (1). But it seems pretty clear to me that whatever principle *does* explain why the δ-move is cheating will also unmask c as a cheater, too.

SD: Perhaps, though I'm uncertain about the matter. Still, I agree that the burden is on the functorese generalist to explain the difference between her view and the *δ*-user.

In any case, let's leave that issue for others to pursue. For we're only talking about *functorese* generalism because you said that it is a view that avoids the two worries—of logical double-counting and the idler's revenge—that you raised for *algebraic* generalism. And I think those worries have replies.

JT: Do tell.

SD: Start with the idler's revenge. Your argument involved two claims. First, that the properties and relations (henceforth, the properties) of algebraic generalism are idlers. And second, that if they're idlers, then algebraic generalism is no better off than individualism with regards to idlers. I think there is room to resist both claims.

Start with the first. This claim has wider applicability, so put the issue of individualism versus algebraic generalism down for a moment. And let us distinguish a property from its causal role. The causal role of a property P might be defined by taking the laws governing it, conjoining them to form a statement T(P), and then replacing all occurrences of P with a variable, resulting in a predicate T(X). This expresses the second-order property of *causing this* and *being caused by that*, and so on. This is its causal role. Now, in your chapter, you mentioned an argument—inspired by Langton (1998) and Lewis (2009)—that we can know that some property or other fills the mass-role, but we cannot know *which* property it is.

JT: That's right. The rough argument is that we can't tell the difference between our world and one just like it except that mass and charge have 'switched roles'. So the property itself (e.g. mass) is 'hidden' behind its causal role in much the same way that a fundamental individual is, according to you, hidden behind its properties.

SD: I like this argument. At least, I find it convincing with regards to so-called 'theoretical' properties like mass and charge. But not for so-called 'observable' properties like red and blue. If one switches these latter, so that anything red becomes blue (and vice-versa), the difference is arguably discernible!

JT: I'll grant that if by 'observable' properties we mean *phenomenal* properties. (Lewis [2009: 217] did, too, in a way.) I'm less confident this holds for other sorts of 'observables,' but I won't fuss about that.

SD: And I'll grant that these theoretical properties are idlers, as you argue. Then if idlers are a vice, the natural reaction is to *do to theoretical properties what the generalist does to individuals*. The view would be that all facts about the property are grounded in facts about their causal role (where this role might involve how it interacts with observable properties). This is 'causal structuralism' about properties.[1]

Call a property a *quiddity* if it is not grounded in its causal role. What the Langton-Lewis argument shows is that quiddities are idlers. Causal structuralism rejects quiddities, and so rejects what was shown to be an idler.

So we have an idler argument against quiddities. And (returning to individuals), we have an idler argument against fundamental individuals. To be rid of *all* idlers, then, one might endorse generalism and causal structuralism together! The technical details of this kind of view are not yet worked out, so I cannot say that I endorse it. But since I think that idlers are a vice, I am eager to see it developed.

JT: Wait. This anti-idler crusade is pushing us much farther than I thought we wanted to go. Suppose I'm right that the only 'observable' properties are phenomenal properties. If so, then you end up with a view where everything is grounded in phenomenal properties, bringing us dangerously close to phenomenalism or neo-Berkelean idealism. I thought the argument against individuals was supposed to stem from principles fairly uncontroversial to scientific realists; if the principles get us phenomenalism, they seem pretty controversial after all. I'm inclined to reject the argument before I let it push me to phenomenalism.

SD: Well, it's not clear that that's the right description of the resulting view! But even if it is, the principle only tells us to dispense with idlers *when all else is equal*. So if at some point along the road the resulting view violates some other principle you hold dear—epistemic conservativism, or some principle that leads to realism—then stop. I'm eager to explore where the argument against idlers leads, but if you aren't, we needn't disagree on the case of individuals.

JT: I'm not so sure. Suppose you dispense with fundamental individuals because they are idlers, but go no further. Then, as we agreed earlier, the generalist view you endorse quantifies over quiddities. If you concede that these are idlers, then the view is just as lousy with idlers as the original individualist view. This is the idlers' revenge.

SD: Yes, the generalist view under discussion does have *one* kind of idler: the quiddities. So it isn't perfect. But the corresponding individualist view has *two* kinds of idlers: quiddities *and* individuals. With respect to the principle that idlers are a vice, the generalist does better.

JT: Fair point. But I was thinking the individualist shouldn't have the quiddities. She should be a nominalist, at least at the fundamental level: There are fundamental facts such as "x is negatively charged," but none such as "x has the quiddity *negative charge*". *This* individualist theory only has one kind of idler, the individuals, since it has dispensed with the quiddities.

SD: That's an interesting move, but I'm not sure it works. Granted, your nominalist only *quantifies* over one kind of idler, the individuals. But the other kind of idler remains. It's just that now it shows up in her *ideology*.

To see the point, consider two theories, T1 and T2. Both are theories of Newtonian space and imply that absolute velocity is real. The only difference is that T1 is platonistic and quantifies over absolute velocities, while T2 is nominalistic. T2 contains a host of predicates, one for each absolute velocity, but no reference to anything that is an absolute velocity.

Now T1 contains an idler: absolute velocity. Focusing just on undetectability for brevity, the idea (recall) is that T1 implies that there is a genuine difference between physical systems which differ only in facts about the absolute velocities of things, and that since those physical systems are indiscernible, those facts about absolute velocity are undetectable (see my chapter, section 2, for details). But if T1 implies this, T2 does too: the fact that T2 is nominalistic doesn't change the fact that there is a genuine difference between these indiscernible systems. So if T1 contains idlers, T2 does too. The difference is just that T2 does not *quantify* over the idlers. The idleness resides in T2's ideology, not its ontology.

The same goes for the individualist you just mentioned. She replaces each quiddity with a predicate, so she no longer *quantifies* over idlers. But the idleness now resides in her ideology, in the predicates she introduced. So she still has two kinds of idlers. The algebraic generalist has only one, so she does better *vis-à-vis* idlers.

JT: I see what you mean. But there's still a point to be made in the ball-park. One bad thing about individualism is that it has 'one fact too many': the general facts '$(\exists x)Fx$', which do the real explanatory work, *and* the individualistic facts 'Fa', which don't do anything but ground the general facts. Algebraic generalism also has one fact too many: the general facts '$(\exists x)\text{Obtains}(x)$', which do the real explanatory work, *and* the quidditistic facts '$\text{Obtains}(p)$', which only get us the general fact. If the individualist is a nominalist, she has her individualistic fact 'Fa', but (by virtue of her nominalism) no general fact like '$(\exists X)Xa$'.

So even though her predicate 'F' is an idler, it doesn't make a fact too many.

These 'facts-too-many' seem epistemically odd to me in their own distinctive way, and maybe that was making me confuse them with your idlers. But I think the facts-too-many are a vice one way or another, and we should try to avoid them if we can. Algebraic generalism gets rid of some of these, but at the cost of introducing new ones.

SD: That's interesting, I hadn't seen that. But if I understand you, *both* your nominalist individualist and my algebraic generalist have a fact too many, though different ones in each case: the individualist has her individualistic facts, the algebraic generalist has her facts about quiddities. To be clear, I don't see why having a fact too many (in your sense) is a vice. But even if it is, the two theories fare equally with respect to it.

JT: Well, both theories have facts-too-many, but it's not clear to me that they do equally well as a result. Some vices are worse than others, and some *instances* of a vice are worse than others. Reasonable people might think that quiddities as facts-too-many are worse than individuals as facts-too-many.

SD: Perhaps, though I don't see why. Still, suppose there were some reason to think that quiddities as facts-too-many are worse than individuals as facts-too-many. Then the question would be whether this cost is worth the benefit of dispensing with idlers.

JT: Right. And that's relevant to how I was thinking about the logical duplication objection, too. That objection held that the algebraic generalist needs extra logical machinery. For example, where the individualist just uses regular conjunction—i.e. the sentential connective—the algebraic generalist uses that *plus* a distinct conjunctive device that operates on properties. I wasn't thinking that this excess structure is *idle*, but that it is *excess*. The individualist kills two birds with one stone, but the algebraic generalist kills one with two. The excess seems like a cost.

SD: If you're right, then as before, the question is whether this cost is worth the benefit of dispensing with idlers.

JT: So let's talk about whether the costs are worth it. Let's set aside the cost of having a fact-too-many, since we're not agreed about whether algebraic generalism does worse in that respect. Then the situation is this. My nominalist has two kinds of idlers, but no logical duplication. And your algebraic generalist has one fewer kind of idler, but logical duplication. Both theories have their vice. Which vice is worse?

SD: This sort of question is notoriously difficult, and I doubt we can settle it here. But I'm inclined to think that your idlers are the more serious vice. Admittedly, philosophers often emphasize the value in *ontological and ideological simplicity*—on getting by with "fewer primitives"—and logical duplication is bad in that regard. But I'm struck by episodes in scientific history in which idlers are rejected even when the resulting theory is less simple in this sense. To see this, consider a Newtonian theory formulated four-dimensionally. Here acceleration can be defined using two primitives: spatial and temporal distance. This theory has an idler in absolute velocity, but to dispense with it, one moves to a Neo-Newtonian theory which needs *three* primitives to define acceleration: spatial and temporal distance *plus* the affine connection. In a Neo-Newtonian structure, this latter is not determined by the former two and so must be added by hand. So this move sacrifices ideological simplicity while dispensing with an idler, yet the consensus is that the cost is worth it. Analogously, if I need extra logical primitives to dispense with other idlers, I'll take them.

Are the cases really analogous? It seems so to me, but there is room to disagree and no room to make my case. So I'll finish by emphasizing how much in general we value rejecting idlers. For notice that rejecting them often results in a *radical* revision of pretheoretic belief. This is easy to forget in the case of absolute velocity, familiar as we are to doing without it. But remember, rejecting absolute velocity implies that there is *no fact of the matter* as to whether I am in the same place I was a moment ago! This is a radical revision of pretheoretic belief about place and motion. Whatever is motivating it must be a weighty consideration indeed, and I believe that it is motivated by the drive to reject idlers.

JT: I suspect when it comes to metaphysical theorizing I put more weight on 'philosophical' virtues than you do. Since that's a preference I also can't hope to defend here, I won't even try.

But let me note that my complaints about logical duplication were supposed to go beyond vague philosophical worries about ideological simplicity. Scientists want theories without idlers, but they also want theories that *unify* phenomena. For instance, Einstein originally developed special relativity in an attempt to unify disparate accounts of certain electromagnetic phenomena, and one of general relativity's virtues is that it subsumes gravitation to inertial motion. In each case, the theory takes phenomena previously thought to be separate and shows them to be ultimately the same thing. That's seen as a virtue. I was thinking logical duplication exhibited the vice corresponding to this virtue: it treated phenomena we previously thought unified as fundamentally disparate. So I was thinking the logical duplication a vice of the sort even scientists wouldn't like.

Of course, even if *that's* right, it still leaves us wondering which vice is worse. I'm not aware of science ever becoming *less* unified in order to get rid of idlers; nor am I aware of it ever introducing idlers to aid unification. Without clear cases to fall back on, it's not obvious how to settle the issue.

SD: Yes, unification is certainly a weighty virtue! I wasn't seeing logical duplication as a violation of unification in quite that sense, but it's a fascinating idea.

In any event, we agree that the question of how to weigh these vices is difficult, unsettled, and vital.

Note

1. See Shoemaker (1980) and Hawthorne (2001) for discussions of causal structuralism. Ney (2007) argues that if one is moved by the Langton-Lewis argument, one should be moved to endorse something like causal structuralism.

References

Hawthorne, John. 2001. "Causal Structuralism." *Philosophical Perspectives* 15: 361–378.

Langton, Rae. 1998. *Kantian Humility: Our Ignorance of Things in Themselves*. Oxford: Oxford University Press.

Lewis, David. 2009. "Ramseyan Humility". In David Braddon-Mitchell and Robert Nola (eds.), *Conceptual Analysis and Philosophical Naturalism*, 203–222. Cambridge, MA: MIT Press.

Ney, Alyssa. 2007. "Physicalism and Our Knowledge of Intrinsic Properties." *Australasian Journal of Philosophy* 85: 41–60.

Shoemaker, Sydney. 1980. "Causality and Properties." In Peter van Inwagen (ed.), *Time and Cause*, 109–135. Dordrecht: Springer.

PART **II**

Is There an Objective Difference between Essential and Accidental Properties?

CHAPTER **3**

Are There Essential Properties? No[1]

MEGHAN SULLIVAN

1. Hardcore Essentialism

Here is a story you might imagine hearing while touring a natural history exhibit:

> **Metamorphosis:** Once there was a fertilized *Danaus plexippus* egg. Call it "Battra." Battra began to grow, with cells fissioning and becoming more specialized, until Battra became a caterpillar. Two weeks later, Battra formed a chrysalis. After several more weeks, Battra emerged as a Monarch butterfly. Battra lived several more weeks until it was captured and mounted in this case. Over time, Battra's wings grew fragile and disintegrated. Lepidopterists replaced parts of the wings with silk. Then Battra's thorax deteriorated. Piece by piece it was replaced with modeling clay. Now Battra is on display here.

The metamorphosis story is intelligible. There is no sentence where meanings obviously shift or fail. It doesn't commit pragmatic errors. Still, we might wonder whether it (or any story of radical change like it) could be true. This takes us into the territory of metaphysics. We might have thought, for instance, that any organic object is *essentially* organic: it could not exist without being organic. But if Battra is essentially organic, then the story is misleading—at some point in its transformation, Battra does not survive.

There is a long tradition of distinguishing properties based on whether they are essential to their bearers or merely accidental. The main idea can be

45

grasped with a metaphor. Imagine reality as a pegboard, with pegs representing individual objects (like Battra) and rubber bands representing their properties (like being organic). Some essentialists think some bands are "glued" to their bearers—the only way to stop the peg from instantiating the property is to remove the peg entirely. Distinguish this *individual* essentialism from *kind* essentialism, the view that there are necessary connections between some properties—i.e. anything gold essentially has atomic number 79. For kind essentialists, the glue holds between bands. This chapter will be concerned with individual essentialism.

The simplistic picture can be made more precise. Here is a view which I will call *Hardcore Essentialism*:

There is some object o and some property P such that:

(i)   o has P;
(ii) if o exists, o must have P (without qualification); and
(iii) P is a qualitative and discriminating property of o.

The first condition is straightforward, but (ii) and (iii) need elaboration.

The 'must' in (ii) expresses a distinctive kind of metaphysical necessity—a necessity that is invariant and broader than mere logical necessity. If a hardcore essentialist says that Battra is essentially organic, he means Battra is organic in every possible world in which it exists. Compare that to the claim that Battra must be organic, *given that it has a body*. This only entails that in every world where Battra has a body, Battra is organic. Condition (ii) can be stated more precisely using modal logic. The hardcore essentialist thinks there are true instances of the following schema: for some property P, $\exists x \Vdash (\exists y(y = x) \to Px)$. Claims like (ii) are *de re* modal claims—they ascribe a modal status to particular objects (like Battra) rather than to sentences or propositions. Here $\Vdash$ captures the distinctive kind of metaphysical necessity.

Condition (iii) distinguishes hardcore essentialism from other theories about the modal connection between objects and properties. A *qualitative* property is a property that more than one object can instantiate. Some philosophers think objects have "haecceities" or "thinnesses"— non-qualitative properties that pick out a particular object and are had only by that object. For instance, we might think President Obama has the property of being Obama. If objects have haecceities, then it seems they must have them.[2] A *discriminating* property is a property that one or more objects can fail to instantiate. Some properties are necessary to their bearers but not discriminating, for instance being self-identical or being such that 2 + 2 = 4. Debates over these properties are important, but considering them would take us too far afield of the main projects in this chapter.

There is a further reason to set aside haecceities and non-discriminating properties. Some philosophers are happy to accept conditions (i)–(iii) as *necessary* conditions for P being an essential property of o, but they deny that they are jointly sufficient. On the more demanding view, an essential property characterizes the underlying nature or gives the real definition of its bearer.[3] For instance, in addition to having the property of being organic whenever it exists, Battra also has the property of being the sole member of Battra's singleton set whenever it exists. But the former property seems more worthy than the latter of being called part of Battra's essence. To account for these differences, *harder-core* essentialists (as I will call them) insist on another condition for essentiality:

(iv) P is the real nature of o (or a part of the real nature of o).[4]

This condition siphons out properties that may happen to be modally glued to their bearers but are nevertheless somehow derivative.

I've described what hardcore essentialists believe. But why believe hardcore essentialism? Three prominent motivations have been given for hardcore (and harder-core) essentialism. In the next section, I will survey these motivations, identifying their key assumptions. Then I will describe why I find these defenses unconvincing.

2. Motivations

Why do we need any arguments for hardcore essentialism? You might think it is just obvious that any particular butterfly is essentially organic. Clearly, essence talk is widespread and can be useful to sort properties as essential or accidental. What is open to debate is whether hardcore essentialism is the best explanation of these practices.

2.1. Explaining semantic intuitions

One prominent defense of hardcore essentialism comes from intuitions about reference.[5] Consider:

Andy has some water, s, and its actual chemical structure is H_2O. Is it possible that Andy could have the very same sample of water, even if its chemical structure were not H_2O? Consider a possible world where Andy has a sample of liquid with almost all of the same qualitative properties as s (clear, flavorless, life-sustaining . . .) except Andy discovers it has a different chemical structure, XYZ. Which is a better description of this world?

(a) In this world, s is XYZ rather than H_2O.
(b) In this world, Andy has something very similar to—but not the same as—s.
(b) seems like a better description than (a). If some substance is not H_2O, there is just no way it is the same sample of water.

Compare this to a different case:

Andy has some orange juice, j, and it is actually sold by Trader Joe's. Is it possible Andy could have the very same sample of juice, even if it were not sold by Trader Joe's? Consider a possible world where Andy has a sample of liquid with all of the same qualitative properties as j (orange, sweet, acidic . . .) except Andy discovers it is sold by a different company, Whole Foods. Which is a better description of this world?

(c) In this world, j is sold by Whole Foods.
(d) In this world, Andy has something very similar to—but not the same as—j.
(c) seems like a more accurate description. Any given sample of juice could be sold by different retailers.

If we are unable to describe a possible world where an object exists while lacking a particular property, then that property is essential to the object. If we are able to describe a world where the same object lacks the property, then the property is not essential. We are unwilling to describe a possible world where the sample of water exists but lacks the property of being H_2O. So being H_2O is essential to the sample. Similar arguments can be given for any chemical microstructure property. Chemical microstructure properties are qualitative and discriminating properties. So hardcore essentialism is true. Call this the *semantic motivation* for essentialism. It appeals to our beliefs about whether the same name ("s" or "j") can pick out the same object in worlds where the properties of the potential referent vary. The crucial assumption of the semantic motivation is that we ought to take our beliefs about reference seriously as a guide to essence.

2.2. Grounding persistence conditions

A second route to hardcore essentialism connects it with our beliefs about change. In 1775, Benjamin Franklin was promoted to French Ambassador. He lost some professional properties when he ceased to be the Postmaster General.

Happily, it seems Franklin continued to exist after the change. In 1790, Franklin contracted pleurisy. He lost some of his organic properties when he ceased to live. Unhappily, it seems he also ceased to exist at this change. How do we explain the changes an object will or will not survive? A natural answer is by appealing to the object's essential properties. Objects can gain and lose accidental properties, but they never survive a change in their essential properties. Facts about essences thus appear to serve an important role in explaining facts about persistence. Indeed, many philosophers have thought that the best solution to the paradoxes of persistence would involve offering a theory of essential properties.

Here is one way to make this reasoning more precise. According to the *persistence motivation* for essentialism, many objects have mind-independent, absolute persistence conditions. Persistence conditions require some kind of ground. Facts about essences are the best candidate for the grounds of persistence conditions. Because there are many examples of persistence conditions which are qualitative and discriminating (i.e. Franklin's *being alive*), the essences which ground persistence are also qualitative and discriminating. Thus, hardcore essentialism is true.[6] The crucial assumptions of the persistence motivation are (1) that we should take our beliefs about persistence seriously as guides to essence, and (2) that persistence conditions require some kind of grounding.

2.3. Methodology of metaphysics

The third route to hardcore essentialism I've already hinted at. Observation can tell us a great deal about the interesting properties of things, but certain kinds of property ascriptions seem "deeper" than others. Consider the following pairs of (true), general property ascriptions:

(1) Electron e is a particle whose upper limit radius is 10^{-22} meters.
(2) Electron e is a negatively charged particle.
(3) Barack Obama is disposed to don attire.
(4) Barack Obama is a thinking animal.
(5) Molecule w is the sole member of $\{w\}$.
(6) Molecule w is composed of two hydrogen atoms bonded with one oxygen atom.

The claims in (1), (3), and (5) are all true, but they do not go very far in capturing what it is to be that electron, man, or molecule. In contrast, the claims in (2), (4), and (6) seem to better explain their subjects. Dating back to Aristotle, there is a tendency to understand metaphysics as the branch of philosophy which seeks explanations like (2), (4), and (6). As Kit Fine describes it, "One of the central concerns of metaphysics is with the identity of things, with what they are. But the metaphysician is not interested in every property of the objects under consideration . . . What is it about a property which makes it bear, in the metaphysically significant sense of the phrase, on what an object is? It is in answer to this question that appeal is naturally made to the concept of essence. For what appears to distinguish the intended properties is that they are essential to their bearers."[7]

On the Neo-Aristotelian view, real natures play a central role in distinguishing good metaphysical theories from bad ones. So real natures are methodologically indispensable. If there are real natures, then presumably they are properties such that, if an object has them, it must have them. Many purported examples of real natures are qualitative and discriminating properties. So hardcore essentialism is true. Call this the *methodological motivation* for essentialism.

3. Questioning the Motivations

Are these motivations convincing? I think the assumptions underlying each are questionable, and taken together they offer (at best) a disjoint picture of what essential properties are like. More importantly, questioning the motivations for hardcore essentialism can point the way toward alternative accounts of what we are doing when we classify properties as essential or accidental.

Consider the semantic motivation first. The water-XYZ thought experiment which drives this argument is not without detractors.[8] Objections to the semantic motivation are typically epistemological—the semantic case uses intuitions about conceivability and reference to motivate essentialism, but it is hard to say what exactly happens when we try to conceive of worlds where a sample of water is not H_2O. I won't repeat these epistemological objections here, but rather focus on objections that more directly target the assumption that our ways of referring reveal essentialist commitments.

Here is a tempting intuition about names—they persist in referring, even when the referent of a name has undergone radical change. The simplest case of this is names for past objects. When Benjamin Franklin died of pleurisy, the name "Franklin" did not cease to refer. Statements such as "Franklin founded the University of Pennsylvania" continue to be meaningful and true. And without much reflection, this seems true of names: anytime a name refers, it has a referent. What's the referent of "Franklin"? Well, it seems it is Franklin. So— if we are taking naive semantic intuitions seriously as a guide to essence—it seems that it is *not* essential to Franklin that he be alive, since he is not alive, but is still a referent of the name "Franklin."[9]

Or consider the ways we can seemingly use a name to track an object through a transformation. In the Metamorphosis story from Section 1, we named an egg, then described a series of gradual changes using that name. At the end of the series was a mostly inorganic object resembling a butterfly.

While the best metaphysical description of the story is a subject of considerable debate, unreflective semantic intuitions lead us to think there is a shared referent of "Battra" at each step in the description—presumably Battra. I suspect we could tell a metamorphosis story for any candidate hardcore essentialist claims. We just need to be able to describe the object undergoing a series of gradual changes. The hardcore essentialist should presumably claim that, in metamorphosis stories, the name words fail to co-refer when the object loses an essential property. He must then offer an error theory for why we mistakenly think reference persists in these cases. But any such error theory will undermine the semantic motivation for essentialism, which assumes we ought to take our beliefs about reference at face value.[10]

Perhaps hardcore essentialists could respond to these challenges by distancing themselves from the semantic motivation. What about the persistence and methodological arguments? Here hardcore essentialists can preserve one motivation but only at the expense of either repudiating the other or denying an attractive assumption about existence. Let me explain.

I assume with many metaphysicians that existence is an all-or-nothing matter. The sense of existence of interest to metaphysics is not susceptible of vagueness.[11] Because existence is an all-or-nothing matter, persistence is also an all-or-nothing matter: for any given object undergoing a change of properties, it either survives the change or it does not. If survival is all-or-nothing, then the properties that account for the persistence conditions of objects must not be susceptible of vagueness. Why? Because if they were susceptible of vagueness, then some persistence conditions would be vague, and so some existence would be vague. To illustrate, compare the following two statements of persistence conditions for a given teapot, t:

P1) If t is shattered, t will not survive.
P2) If t loses 10^{-22} or more of its molecules, t will not survive.

P1 is hopelessly vague, because there are many indeterminate cases of shattering. If a teapot breaks into seven pieces, has it shattered? Thirty-seven pieces? P2 is less vague (though, of course, the losing relation among a teapot and its parts is susceptible of some vagueness). Determinacy of existence pressures us to think that objects have very precise persistence conditions. So if the hardcore essentialist is right that we need essences to serve as the persistence conditions of objects, then these essences must also be very precise properties, more like P2.

But according to the methodological motivation, we should believe in essences because they are the proper subject matter for metaphysical explanations. The kinds of properties that make for good explanations tend to be general properties, highly susceptible of vagueness. Compare two possible real definitions of a given teapot, t:

D1) To be t is to be a small vessel for pouring hot water.
D2) To be t is to be a small vessel for pouring hot water that has not lost
10^{-22} or more of its molecules.

If essences are the kinds of properties which characterize the real nature of their bearer and contribute to good explanations, then D1 seems more likely than D2 to be a true essence ascription. But D1 is much *less* suited to be a persistence condition then D2. D1 is much more susceptible of vagueness. A similar kind of argument can be given for other kinds of essence ascriptions. We might think any particular organism is essentially an organism (when giving its real definition) but acknowledge that being an organism is hopelessly vague. We might think any given water molecule is essentially composed of H_2O while acknowledging that molecular composition is susceptible of vagueness.

The essentialist has options for accounting for this role incompatibility. First, he might insist that the properties which serve as persistence essences are distinct from the properties that serve as real natures. In this case, he must admit that the different motivations for essentialism do not both support a single theory of essential properties. Indeed, the metaphysician's term "essence" is ambiguous between properties that play these different roles. Second, he can give up the assumption that existence is always determinate. Finally, he might promote one of the motivations for essentialism and deny the other.

But for me, these challenges raise the question of whether we can do without modal glue entirely. The resulting picture of reality would be simpler—we would no longer postulate an absolute distinction among objects' properties. And, as I'll argue, the resulting picture may better account for the role that essence ascriptions play in our everyday thought. But if we mean to deny hardcore essentialism, we need some other theory of why it seems so attractive to categorize properties as essential and accidental. What are we doing when we ascribe essences?

4. Meaning-Relative Essentialism

Let's say an *anti-essentialist* is anyone who denies at least one of the three conditions of hardcore essentialism. The most obvious target is condition (ii): if o exists, o must have P without qualification. (Only an extremist would deny (i) or (iii), since this is tantamount to denying that objects have qualitative and discriminating properties.) There are two ways that an anti-essentialist might object to condition (ii). First, she might object that the condition, as explained, makes no sense. W.V.O. Quine famously presses this kind of objection to essentialism—arguing that all *de re* modal ascriptions are unintelligible.[12] Call any view which denies the coherence of (ii) *pure anti-essentialism*.

Pure anti-essentialism is tough to defend. Many *de re* modal claims seem perfectly intelligible (at least as intelligible as any topic in metaphysics).[13]

A second way to object to (ii) is to admit that we can make sense of essence ascriptions, but insist that they aren't true without qualification. When we say that an object has a property essentially, we aren't asserting some absolute fact about a connection between the object and that property; rather, we are asserting some qualified fact about the connection between the object and the property. More recent kinds of anti-essentialism pursue this approach. On these views, we interpret "x must have P" as an instance of the following schema:

Relative Essentialism: For some property P and some parameter R, $\exists x \leftarrow R (\exists y (y = x) \rightarrow Px)$.[14]

According to the relative essentialists, there is no one absolute modal connection between an object and any of it properties. Rather, the connection between an object and its property is only deemed "essential" relative to some parameter. How we fill out parameter R determines what kind of relative essentialist you are. To date, the most popular version of relative essentialism holds that something has a property essentially relative to a convention for referring to and individuating objects. For instance, a given sample of water is essentially H_2O given that, in our language, chemical microstructure properties are the proper way to individuate samples of water. If we had a different language that used some other set of properties (say, color and viscosity) to individuate samples of water, then water would not be essentially H_2O, because samples that are not H_2O can have the same color and viscosity as water. Call this view *meaning-relative essentialism* since, according to the view, essential property ascriptions only hold relative to semantic or metasemantic facts.[15] (The view is also sometimes called "conventionalism.") Using the schema above, the meaning-relative essentialist understands the "must" in condition (ii) as follows: given semantic convention C, for some property P, $\exists x \leftarrow C (\exists y (y = x) \rightarrow Px)$. Substitute a different convention in the schema, and the result is a different essence ascription, which may be false given the particular convention.

There are some problems for meaning-relative essentialism. First, in making essences semantically dependent, it seems that the meaning-relative essentialist also makes *existence* semantically dependent. The meaning-dependent essentialist insists that Battra is essentially organic only relative to a way of individuating butterflies. When most of Battra's body has been replaced by inorganic parts, does Battra still exist? If our convention imposes an organic requirement on picking out Battra, then it doesn't survive. If our convention imposes some other requirement for picking out Battra (say that it looks like a butterfly), then Battra survives. So it seems Battra's existence at a time depends on semantic facts.[16] The same holds for any other object. But this is absurd.[17]

Anti-essentialism is often taken to be a fast-track to ontological anti-realism, and many meaning-relative essentialists are happy to accept this result. But I don't think the meaning-relative essentialist is *forced* to adopt anti-realism. Behind this objection is an assumption that the persistence motivation for essentialism is sound. If essences are semantically dependent, and essences ground persistence, then persistence conditions are semantically dependent. If persistence conditions are semantically dependent, and persistence conditions ground facts about existence, then existence is also semantically dependent. But existence is not semantically dependent, so neither are essences. Or so the objection goes. In response to this objection, the realist meaning-relative essentialist would do well to deny that persistence conditions are grounded in facts about essences. There may be semantically independent facts about which objects exist, which properties they instantiate, and how long they have persisted or will persist. But these facts are grounded in something other than facts about essences, or perhaps they are grounded in nothing at all. I don't think that abandoning the persistence motivation is a great cost since, as we've seen, even hardcore essentialists are pressured to divide the persistence and methodological motivations.

Other problems for meaning-relative essentialism are more difficult to answer. For instance, the theory also seems far too permissive. Suppose we adopt a language with the convention of referring to and individuating objects based solely on their locations. This would be a bizarre convention, but it is a potential one nonetheless. At 10:00 am, President Obama is a human sitting in his chair in the Oval Office. At 10:30 am, a poached egg is in the chair. Is there an object that is Obama at 10:00 am and the egg at 10:30? It seems natural to think Obama *just could not* become a poached egg (let alone in half an hour). No sensible account of essence and accident ascriptions allows for contexts in which "Obama could be a poached egg" is true.[18] But there is at least one convention—the one described above—such that Obama's essence does not preclude him from being a poached egg. If that convention were in play, "Obama could be a poached egg" would be true. So, it seems, the conventionalist must deny that there is an absolute or unqualified limit on what Obama could become. The (sensible) permissiveness of semantic conventions leads to an objectionably permissive anti-essentialism.[19]

Finally, meaning-relative essentialism fails to give a convincing theory of why we care so much about essential properties. Actual semantic conventions are in an important sense arbitrary. They evolved to solve coordination and communication problems, but in many cases one convention could be just as useful as another. Suppose we had a different convention for referring to and re-identifying people—say, by being the same person disposed to don attire rather than being the same thinking animal. We could use such a convention to solve coordination problems. But then Obama would be essentially disposed to don attire but not essentially be a thinking animal. So why think there is anything "deep" to Obama being a thinking animal? Arbitrarily adopted semantic conventions cannot account for why some true property ascriptions are more explanatorily valuable than others. So meaning-relative essentialism fails to account for one of the main ways we use essentialist discourse, namely, to distinguish good explanations.

I think the meaning-relative essentialists are right in denying (ii). They are also right in thinking that when we ascribe essential properties to an object, the ascriptions are context sensitive. Where they go wrong is in choosing the relevant parameter R. There is a better form of anti-essentialism available.

5. Explanation-Relative Essentialism

There are at least three features I want in a theory of how and why we classify properties as essential or accidental.

First, I want a theory that is consistent with realism. In particular, it should be consistent with the view that the existence of many objects and many of their properties does not depend on our concepts or semantic conventions. As we've seen, meaning-relative essentialists struggle on this point unless they deny that essences ground persistence conditions.

Second, I want a theory that does justice to the purpose of essential property attributions. At the very least, the theory should be consistent with the view that there are better and worse theories of objects and their properties, that better theories ascribe essences and worse theories do not, and that and these differences in explanatory value do not arise arbitrarily. As we've seen, meaning-relative essentialism and weaker forms of hardcore essentialism struggle on this front.

Third, I want the theory to explain the apparent context-sensitivity of essence attributions while still being consistent with the view that there are absolute limits on the properties an object could have. So the theory should explain why the correctness of essential property attributions might sometimes vary across contexts, but there should be no context where President Obama is only accidentally human. As we've seen, hardcore essentialism flatly denies there is any context-sensitivity in true essence attributions. Meaning-relative essentialism explains the context-sensitivity of essence attributions, but it allows too much freedom.

I think the best way to satisfy these three desiderata is to employ the framework of a relativist theory, but instead of looking to semantic conventions to provide parameter R, prioritize the role that essences play in good explanations. Before explicitly stating the relativist theory I support, it will be helpful to lay out some assumptions about the nature of explanation which will underwrite the theory.

An explanation is an answer to a "why" question. Why did Joe's cancer metastasize? Why did Scotland's recession end while England's didn't? An *explanatory framework* is a set of norms for giving a good explanation in a particular domain. For instance, there is a framework for good explanations in medicine. If a physician wants to explain why a particular tumor metastasized, any good explanation will reference changes in the extracellular matrix surrounding the tumor. A good medical explanation need not describe the quantum state of a particular electron orbiting a hydrogen atom in the tumor. But a good quantum explanation might very well focus on the spin state of atoms in the system. Different domains of inquiry come with their own explanatory frameworks—medicine, quantum mechanics, economics, logic, theology, astronomy, astrology, and so on. I further assume (more controversially) that there are objective norms governing some explanatory frameworks. We discover these norms as a good science develops. Degenerate systems of inquiry such as astrology are degenerate, in part, because there are no objective norms to govern their explanations.[20] What accounts for the objectivity of these norms and how do we come to know them? Here there is flexibility in the theory, and presumably we should take our guidance from the best theories of objective explanation in the sciences.

According to *explanation-relative essentialism*, an essence ascription is true relative to an explanatory framework if and only if an object is ascribed that property in any good explanation of that type, and there are objective norms governing explanatory frameworks in that domain. A property is only essential to an object relative to an explanatory framework, and true essence ascriptions may vary across frameworks. Even more precisely, explanation-relative essentialism holds:

An object o is essentially P relative to framework E iff:

(i)   o has P;
(ii) in any good explanation of type E which involves o, o has P; and
(iii) there are objective norms governing explanations of type E.

We can use this framework to define accidental properties.
An object o is accidentally P relative to E iff:

(i) o has P;
(ii) o is not essentially P relative to E;

Outside of an explanatory framework, an object's properties can be considered neither essential nor accidental.[21]

It is easiest to understand how the theory works by applying it to some very simple models.

Case 1: Physics. I'm offering an explanation for why some coin, c, completes an electrical circuit. c has the properties of conducting electricity and of being a unit of account in a financial market. Any good physical explanation of why c completes a circuit will cite its conductivity. Suppose there are objective norms underlying physical explanations. Then it is true that c essentially conducts electricity in my explanatory context. But c is only accidentally a unit of account, since a good physical explanation involving c need not cite c's economic properties.

Case 2: Economics. I'm offering an explanation why c is worth ten cents. Any good economic explanation of why c is worth ten cents will cite its property of being a unit of account in a market. Suppose there are objective norms underlying economic explanations. Then c is essentially a unit of account in my explanatory context. But c accidentally conducts electricity, since economics is indifferent to the electrical properties of currency.

Case 3: Astrology. I'm offering an explanation for why John is extroverted, honest, and likely to marry someone born in late December. Suppose John has the property of being born in late December and being a Sagittarian. Any "good" astrological explanation of John's personality and destiny will cite his sun sign. But John is not essentially Sagittarian, since there are no objective norms to underwrite astrological explanations. His astrological sign is, at best, accidental in this context.[22]

This gives a sketch of how explanation-relative essentialism predicts the truth of essence ascriptions. But explanation-relative essentialists may fill in the details in different ways. For instance, some explanation-relative essentialists might suppose that many special sciences are governed by objective norms and are not reducible to one another. Such philosophers might countenance a far wider variety of true essence ascriptions than reductive physicalists. And if there are no objective explanatory norms, then explanation-relative essentialism predicts that there are no true essence ascriptions. Here my aim is to describe the general framework as an alternative to hardcore and meaning-relative essentialism, deferring such issues in implementation to later work.

So how will explanation-relative essentialism address our three desiderata?

First, to preserve realism, the explanation-relative essentialist should use the same strategy I suggested on behalf of the meaning-relative essentialist. Facts about explanatory norms and interests determine facts about essences relative to a context, but facts about essences do not determine persistence conditions. When we ascribe an essence to an object, we are *highlighting* one of its properties and claiming that the property enjoys a certain kind of explanatory indispensability. Whether a coin conducts electricity does not vary with our explanatory interests. But whether that property counts as essential to the coin may well vary.

Second, explanation-relative essentialism gives an account of the relationship between essences and our judgments about good or bad explanations, since essences are defined as *whatever* properties are indispensable to good explanations in that context. But it is not arbitrary which of an object's properties count as essential. Essence ascriptions are correct only insofar as they reflect objective explanatory norms that operate in that context. And it may be the case that some objects must have some properties in *every* explanatory context with objective norms. In this case, we might say that some property is super-essential to its bearer.[23] For example, perhaps in every objective explanatory context, any good explanation which involves President Obama is one in which he is human. In this case, humanity would be super-essential to Obama. Depending on how many objective explanatory contexts there are, explanation-relative essentialism may or may not be very permissive with accidental property attributions. This is a benefit of the theory. Unlike meaning-relative essentialism, explanation-relative essentialism need not (for all we have assumed about explanation) supply any context where Obama is only accidentally human.

Do such essences characterize the methodology of metaphysics? Some might take on the explanation-relative essentialism framework, but still insist that there is an important framework for *metaphysical* explanation, with its own corresponding objective norms. What were formerly thought to be the absolute essences of an object are just the properties that are indispensable to a metaphysical explanation of that object. For example:

> Case 4: Metaphysics. I am offering an explanation for why some object, c, has proper parts. Suppose c has the properties of being extended in space and time and of being an automobile. Any good metaphysical explanation of c's proper parts will cite its extension in space and time. No good metaphysical explanation will cite its being an automobile. Suppose there are objective norms governing metaphysical explanation. Then c is essentially extended but only accidentally an automobile.

On this approach, explanation-relative essentialism resembles harder-core essentialism, but with three differences. First, harder-core essentialists typically assume that facts about essences are needed to ground explanatory norms. The explanation-relative essentialist thinks facts about explanatory norms are prior. This should be taken as a benefit for explanation-relative essentialism: we have a stronger grip on the norms governing good explanations than on what properties are "metaphysically special." Second, the harder-core essentialists assume there is one privileged context of explanation—the metaphysical context—which determines absolute essence ascriptions. The explanation-relative essentialist thinks the metaphysical context is (at best) one among many. It may be part of any good metaphysical explanation involving a coin that it has the properties of being extended. But there may be economic explanations that are indifferent to whether the coin is extended—the explanations would be just as good for the purposes of economics if the coin were not extended in space and time. Whether all explanatory frameworks reduce to the metaphysics framework is a highly contentious issue, and one which the explanation-relative essentialist need not take a stand on. Third, while the harder-core essentialist may think there is a single, exhaustive essential/accidental classification of an object's properties, the explanation-relative essentialist thinks that, outside of a context of explanation, such a classification is incoherent.

To summarize: explanation-relative essentialism gives a theory for why correct essence ascriptions and good explanations tend to go hand in hand. Depending on how conservative one is with objective explanations, it need not be very permissive with accident ascriptions. And it does not merely collapse into harder-core essentialism.

What about the third desiderata—accounting for context-sensitivity of essence ascriptions? Recall the metamorphosis story that began this discussion. Presumably in storytelling contexts, there are very few (perhaps no) objective norms governing explanations and so very few (or no) correct essence ascriptions when we are operating in this context. Thus, we can tell Kafkaesque stories about one thing transforming into another, and explanation-relative essentialism predicts that the story would strike as coherent. If we were entertaining the metamorphosis story in a more restrictive context (say offering zoological explanations about insect life cycles), then the story is no longer coherent, since organisms are never made of inorganic material in zoological theories. We can observe this shiftiness in essence attribution whenever we have a smooth shift involving explanatory contexts that the object and properties might feature in. For instance, the following speeches sound correct . . .

(1) Gold atom g essentially moves more slowly than a photon. Well, not if special relativity is false. (Shift from an SR-based physics framework to a non-SR physics or broadly metaphysical framework.)[24]

(2) Peter is essentially an organism. Well, not if he has an immaterial soul. (Shift from a biological or materialist framework to a dualist's framework.). . . . while (3) sounds bad:

(3) Gold atom g is essentially slower than a photon. Well, not if a many-valued logic is correct. (Shift in context is not smooth, since gold atoms do not typically figure in non-classical logical explanations.)

6. Conclusion

I find explanation-relative essentialism an attractive alternative to hardcore essentialism. It does justice to the connection between essences and good explanation. It is fully consistent with ontological realism. And it does all of this without requiring any "modal glue" in the world. I've only given a programmatic overview of the theory here. But in the absence of better motivations for hardcore essentialism, I think there is much to recommend this anti-essentialist alternative.

Notes

1. This chapter grew out of a Spring 2014 graduate seminar on modality at Notre Dame. I'm grateful to the participants in that seminar and to my co-teacher, Sam Newlands, for advice on drafts and helpful philosophical discussion. I'm also grateful to Peter Finocchiaro and audience members at UC Irvine, Bogazici University, the University of Barcelona and a 2014 Notre Dame faculty colloquium for useful comments on later drafts.
2. For a prominent defender of haecceitistic essentialism, see Plantinga (1974). For criticism of the view, see Adams (1981).
3. For example, Fine (1994). Fine goes further, suggesting that modal necessity (as in condition (ii)) ought to be defined in terms of real natures.
4. L.A. Paul calls this "deep" essentialism. See Paul (2006).
5. See, for instance, Lecture III of Kripke (1980). The Water-XYZ cases come from Putnam (1975), but it is unclear whether Putnam endorses hardcore essentialism rather than some form of meaning-relative essentialism.
6. See, for example, Wiggins (1980), Lowe (2008), and Elder (2011). Or Chapter 4 of Rea (2002).
7. Fine (1994: 1).
8. See Searle (1983), Sidelle (1989), and Thomasson (2007) for criticisms of essentialist conclusions drawn from Twin Earth.
9. B-theorists and other eternalists about past existents will offer a theory of how this could be true—Franklin is still alive in another region of space-time. But this won't vindicate the semantic motivation, since it is implausible to think that our ordinary semantic practices belie any deep eternalist commitments.
10. In a similar vein, Quine argues that there are no meaningful criteria of transworld identity using intuitions about gradual change across worlds. He writes, "our cross-moment identification of bodies turned on continuity of de-placement, distortion, and chemical change. These considerations cannot be extended across worlds, because you can change anything to anything by easy stages through some connecting series of possible worlds." Quine (1976: 861).
11. Lowe (1989: 4). Van Inwagen (1998) and Sider (2011) give some more recent arguments for the univocity of existence. One can endorse the univocity of existence while still admitting it is vague—perhaps by endorsing some kind of metaphysical indeterminacy. But I reject this as well. For more in vagueness and persistence conditions, see Sullivan (2012).
12. Quine (1961).
13. See, for instance, Plantinga (1974).
14. I'm grateful to Sam Newlands for discussion on this way of presenting the issues.
15. Versions of this kind of view can be found in Sidelle (1989). Thomasson (2007) and Thomasson (2010) develop a view where essence attributions reflect linguistic prescriptions for using name words and kind terms. She calls the view "modal normativism."
16. Or metasemantic facts: facts about which conventions have been adopted.
17. Chapter 4 of Rea (2002) uses considerations about grounds of persistence to argue against meaning-relative essentialists. Lowe (2008) uses similar arguments to dispute concept-dependent essentialism.
18. Note that harder-core essentialists seem committed to saying that "Obama is essentially a non-poached egg" is false, since being a non-poached egg is not a good candidate for being a real nature.
19. For a version of this objection, see Paul (2006). She poetically accuses the meaning-relative essentialist of "selling his soul to Quine" (345).

20. Another way to put this is that there are objective laws that back good sciences, but no such laws backing degenerate sciences. The relationship between irreducible laws and objective explanatory norms is an interesting one, which I cannot consider here.
21. This notion of an explanatory framework is irreducibly normative and also supposes that within a framework there are invariant standards for counting some proposition as a good answer to a why question. Compare to more radically contextualist theories of explanation like van Frassen (1988).
22. I say "at best" because being Sagittarian may not be a property at all.
23. Distinguish this from another view called "super-essentialism", the view that every property an object instantiates is essential to the object.
24. Inspired by, but distinct from, Sider's examples in Sider (2011: 181).

References

Adams, Robert Merrihew. 1981. "Actualism and Thisness." *Synthese* 49: 3–41.
Elder, Crawford L. 2011. *Familiar Objects and Their Shadows*. Cambridge: Cambridge University Press.
Fine, Kit. 1994. "Essence and Modality." *Philosophical Perspectives* 8: 1–16.
Kripke, Saul. 1980. *Naming and Necessity*. Cambridge: Harvard University Press.
Lowe, E.J. 1989. *Kinds of Being: A Study of Individuation, Identity, and the Logic of Sortal Terms, volume 10 of Aristotelian Society Series*. Oxford: Basil Blackwell.
Lowe, Jonathan. 2008. "How Are Identity Conditions Grounded?" In Christian Kanzian (ed.), *Persistence*, 73–89. Heusenstamm, Germany: Ontos Verlag.
Paul, L.A. 2006. "In Defense of Essentialism." *Philosophical Perspectives* 20: 333–372.
Plantinga, Alvin. 1974. *The Nature of Necessity*. Oxford: Clarendon Press.
Putnam, Hilary. 1975. "The Meaning of 'Meaning'." *Minnesota Studies in the Philosophy of Science* 7: 131–193.
Quine, W.V. 1961. *From a Logical Point of View*, 2nd edition, 139–159. New York: Harper and Row.
———. 1976. "Worlds Away." *Journal of Philosophy* 73: 859–863.
Rea, Michael C. 2002. *World without Design: The Ontological Consequences of Naturalism*. Oxford: Oxford University Press.
Searle, John R. 1983. *Intentionality: An Essay in Philosophy of Mind*. Cambridge: Cambridge University Press.
Sidelle, Alan. 1989. *Necessity, Essence, and Individuation: A Defense of Conventionalism*. Ithaca, NY: Cornell University Press.
Sider, Theodore. 2011. *Writing the Book of the World*. Oxford: Oxford University Press.
Sullivan, Meghan. 2012. "The Minimal A-Theory." *Philosophical Studies* 158: 149–174.
Thomasson, Amie L. 2007. *Ordinary Objects*. New York: Oxford University Press.
———. 2010. "Modal Normativism and the Methods of Metaphysics." *Philosophical Topics* 35: 135–160.
van Frassen, Bas C. 1988. "The Pragmatic Theory of Explanation." In Jospeh C. Pitt (ed.), *Theories of Explanation*, 136–155. Oxford: Oxford University Press.
van Inwagen, Peter. 1998. "Meta-Ontology." *Erkenntnis* 48: 233–250.
Wiggins, David. 1980. *Sameness and Substance*. Oxford: Basil Blackwell.

CHAPTER 4

Are There Essential Properties? Yes

KRIS McDANIEL AND STEVE STEWARD

1. Introduction

Meghan Sullivan calls *hardcore essentialism* the thesis that there's at least one object and qualitative and discriminating property such that the object must (absolutely and without qualification) have the property if it exists. Although we have qualms about this characterization of hardcore essentialism, we ignore them in what follows, and defend hardcore essentialism as Sullivan characterises it.[1]

Sullivan discusses (and rejects) some interesting but inconclusive arguments for hardcore essentialism. Each argument suggests that we should believe in essential properties because of the explanatory work they can do. But explanatory power does not ultimately provide our reason for accepting hardcore essentialism. Our reason is simply that we can't believe that we could've been poached eggs. But in some sense, each of us can believe the proposition expressed by, 'I could've been a poached egg'; we're essentially not poached eggs, but not essentially non-believers in the possibility of our being poached eggs. More on the subtleties of 'can' in section 3.

None of us could've been a buttered bagel. Nobody believes this simply on the basis of a philosophical argument. It's great if your not possibly being a glass of orange juice explains some semantic phenomenon, or partially explains your persistence conditions, or whatnot. But we don't believe that you couldn't have been a glass of orange juice *because* of what this fact might purportedly explain. And since each of us couldn't have been a Belgian waffle, there's one property—not being a Belgian waffle—that you absolutely must have if you exist. There are many others. So, hardcore essentialism is true.

We stress this because we view the dialectical situation differently than Sullivan. We don't see hardcore essentialism as reasonable to believe only if it's a consequence of a good philosophical argument. Rather, hardcore essentialism is sufficiently plausible to be the default position. And so the onus on the hardcore essentialist is not to provide an argument for the view but is instead to merely respond defensively to arguments against the view. For this reason, we focus on Sullivan's arguments against hardcore essentialism.

2. Essences of Individuals and Essences of Entities in General

Sullivan explicitly restricts her focus on whether hardcore essentialism is true with respect to individuals rather than kinds. We'll be less restrictive, partly because there are entities besides individuals that have essential properties, and partly because it's worth determining to what extent one can have a uniform account of attribution of essential properties to entities in general rather than merely to individuals.

Consider *sounds*. You play a middle C on the piano. This particular sound has accidental features, e.g., that it's heard. But it also has essential features: in general, sounds without volumes are metaphysically impossible. Consider *holes*. This hole in my buttered bagel couldn't have existed without being a hole in something. Holes must have hosts. More exotic entities also have essential features. *Sets* must have the members that they have. *Species* essentially fall under their genera.

We do hardcore essentialism a disservice if we under-emphasise how general the notion of an essential property is, and if we fail to note the number of near obvious truths about essential properties. Not every attribution of essential properties is a near obvious truth, as we'll see in section 3. But the hard-core essentialist needn't settle the harder cases to feel comfortable in her hardcore essentialism, for there are many easy ones to be content with.

Here's why we characterize these essentialists truths as 'near obvious'. Hardcore essentialism is a view about what is absolutely necessary with respect to objects. But whether there's an intelligible notion of absolute necessity is non-obvious. Start with the idea that there are some ways in which things could've gone, and other ways thing could not have gone; this is the distinction between what is absolutely possible and absolutely impossible. Here are three views about the status of the line between the possible and the impossible. View one: it's a fundamental fact that the line is drawn

where it is. View two: it's not a fundamental fact but it's a uniquely privileged fact: there's no other way to divide up possible and impossible worlds
that's at least as fundamental.[2] View three: it is neither fundamental nor
uniquely privileged; there are alternative ways of partitioning the worlds
that are as legitimate as the division in to the absolutely possible and the
absolutely impossible.[3] We incline to either the first or the second view, but
it's not part of hardcore essentialism that either is true: the third view is also
a possibility.

Here's what the hardcore essentialist is committed to: in whatever way
it's absolutely necessary that 2 + 2 = 4, that it's morally wrong to torture
innocent persons for fun, and that possible worlds are not concrete objects
with the same metaphysical status as this universe, it's also absolutely necessary that we're not potato pancakes.[4] There are hard questions about absolute necessity; but these hard questions are about absolute necessity *tout
court* rather than about essential properties specifically. We claim that it's
about as obvious that we absolutely couldn't be glasses of chocolate milk as
it is that 2 + 2 must be 4. Perhaps there are special epistemological worries
about *de re* necessity that don't have analogues in the epistemology of *de
dicto* necessity, but that's consistent with there being near obvious truths
about each.

Given this view of the dialectical situation, our primary job is to reply to
arguments against hardcore essentialism rather than offer positive defences of
it. The remainder of the paper focuses on (in section 3) Sullivan's main arguments against hardcore essentialism and then (in section 4) Sullivan's proposed replacement for genuine essential features.

3. Sullivan's Arguments against Hardcore Essentialism

Sullivan presents several intriguing arguments. We'll focus on three that seem
both central to her case and most challenging to address.

3.1. *The Argument from Hard Cases*

Sullivan starts her chapter with this story about a character named 'Battra' that, according to the story, starts as a fertilized egg, then becomes a
caterpillar, a chrysalis, a monarch butterfly, and finally a mounted instal-
lation partially made of a butterfly corpse and modelling clay. Sullivan's
story is worth contemplating. It describes commonplace changes; it's not
science fiction. This is important, since readers of stories typically are very
concessive to the authors of those stories. If we tell a story in which a prince
becomes a toad, the typical reader will play along even if such a change is

metaphysically impossible; the story is no fun to tell or hear if we let meta-physical scruples get in the way. But with a realistic story, we're less suscep-tible to simply accept what is told.

If we accept Sullivan's story as metaphysically possible exactly as it's told, it seems as if Battra is a counterexample to several views about which essential properties objects have. One view says that organisms are essen-tially alive. Another says that organisms are essentially composed of the same kinds of organic material throughout their timespan. Both of these appear false if the story of Battra is possible. For in the story, Battra exists after its death, and even after its original organic material is replaced by silk and clay.

But pause. The hardcore essentialist could concede that Sullivan's story is metaphysically possible exactly as it's told while denying that it's a counter-example to the two essentialist views just mentioned. For one, the hardcore essentialist could deny that Battra is an organism. On one view about persis-tence through time, *perdurantism*, objects persist through an interval of time T by having temporal parts that correspond to the sub-intervals of T. And, if composition is fully unrestricted, all things compose a whole, regardless of where or when they are.[5] If perdurantism is true and composition is fully unrestricted, then there's an entity that survives exactly the changes Battra is depicted as surviving. But this entity is not an organism; it merely coincides with one for some part of its timespan.[6]

Perdurantism and fully unrestricted composition are compatible with hardcore essentialism. But in what follows, we'll make things harder on our-selves by rejecting (if only for the sake of argument) both views.

With that in mind, let's get clearer about how Sullivan's story is relevant. Is there a good argument from the Battra story against hardcore essentialism? Consider this argument:

1. Battra exists when it's a caterpillar and when it's made of silk and clay.
2. If Battra exists when it's a caterpillar and when it's made of silk and clay, then Battra is not essentially an organism.
3. If hardcore essentialism is true, then Battra is essentially an organism.
4. So, hardcore essentialism is not true.

If Sullivan's story is possible, then premise 1 is true. And in what follows, we won't challenge premise 2. Premise 3 might seem true because 'organisms are essentially organisms' is especially plausible. The hardcore essentialist presum-ably wants to defend some interesting *positive* proposals about the essential features of things. And one might think that this claim must be true if any essentialist claim is.

There are several possible responses.

First, we might reject premise 1 by denying that Sullivan's story is possible. Perhaps Battra goes out of existence when it stops being alive or when it stops being an organism.[7] Either of these options is plausible.

Perhaps this option is unavailable to someone who takes naïve semantic intuitions seriously, since, according to this option, either 'Battra' refers to different entities at different points in the story, or at some time in the story, 'Battra' no longer refers to something that exists at that time. We've already emphasized that we don't take naïve semantic intuition as our guide to essence. In this context, it's not at all clear to us why anyone should. Why take intuitions about *words* as a guide rather than, for example, intuitions about the objects themselves, preferably in conjunction with detailed information gathered from the biological or chemical sciences? (Why prefer the naïve intuitions of someone doing semantics rather than those of a biologist?)

Another response is to deny premise 3. Hardcore essentialism isn't committed to any claim about which objects have which properties essentially. It's just the view that at least one object has at least one property essentially. Maybe Battra doesn't have any essential properties. Maybe Battra has some essential properties other than being organic. Both of these claims are consistent with the claim that we couldn't have been biscuits and gravy. And hence both of these claims are consistent with hardcore essentialism, so we don't have to decide which (if any) properties are essential to Battra to defend hardcore essentialism.

Even though we don't need to decide which essential properties objects have, we'll suggest two plausible views:

Origin Essentialism: everything that has an origin has its origin essentially.[8]
Category Essentialism: everything that belongs to an ontological category belongs to that category essentially.[9]

Neither of these imply that organisms are essentially alive or essentially organisms. And both are consistent with Sullivan's story. Battra never loses its origin or changes ontological category.[10]

Sullivan (p. 51) suggests that, 'we could tell a metamorphosis story for any candidate hardcore essentialist claims. We just need to be able to describe the object undergoing a series of gradual changes'. But it's very hard to produce a plausible metamorphosis story in which its protagonist changes its origin. In order for something to come to have a different origin than it once did, the past would have to change. And it's well known that changing the past is paradoxical. So we doubt that a story like Sullivan's could be developed that would have much intuitive force against origin essentialism. And we don't believe there are good non-story based arguments against origin essentialism either.

Changing one's ontological category is not paradoxical in the way that changing one's origin is. But it seems impossible, at least with respect to a wide variety of ontological categories. Consider this metamorphosis story:

> **Metamorphosis 2**: Once there was a metaphysician named Elizabeth. She started out as an ordinary human organism. Then she transformed from a human into a parade—not a person in a parade, but the event itself. When she finished being a parade, Elizabeth transformed into a new species of *Felinae*: not a new individual member of this biological family, but a new species. Finally, Elizabeth became a set.

This story is much less intelligible than the story about Battra. It's absolutely impossible for an organism to become an event, or a species, or a set. We aren't relying on semantic intuitions at all; we simply can't bring ourselves to believe that Elizabeth (or anyone else) could change in these ways.

Hardcore essentialism is true if either Origin or Category Essentialism is true. No plausible metamorphosis story challenges either Origin or Category Essentialism. So, metamorphosis stories like the one involving Battra don't pose a serious challenge to hardcore essentialism.

We think that the story of Battra does raise an interesting puzzle about what essential properties the character (or characters) of that story in fact have. This is the sort of puzzle that hardcore essentialists ought to think about, and they ought to develop and defend theories that solve it. Perhaps it's an advantage of denying hardcore essentialism that it dissolves such hard puzzles rather than forces us to solve them. Our view though is that reality is sometimes puzzling.

3.2. The Argument from Ben Franklin

The second argument is encapsulated in the following quotation:

> Here is a tempting intuition about names—they persist in referring, even when the referent of a name has undergone radical change. The simplest case of this is names for past objects. When Benjamin Franklin died of pleurisy, the name 'Franklin' did not cease to refer. Statements such as 'Franklin founded the University of Pennsylvania' continue to be meaningful and true. And without much reflection, this seems true of names: anytime a name refers, it has a referent. What's the referent of 'Franklin'? Well, it seems it is Franklin. So—if we are taking naive semantic intuitions seriously as a guide to essence—it seems that it is *not* essential to

Franklin that he be alive, since he is not alive, but is still a referent of the name 'Franklin.'

(Sullivan: 50)

Our response is multifold. First, we remind the reader that we neither rely on intuitions about semantics as our guide to essence, nor on naïve intuitions, but rather accept those intuitions about the objects themselves (rather than their names) that we believe survive critical reflection while maintaining their forcefulness.

Second, we remind the reader that hardcore essentialism does not entail that it's essential to Franklin to be alive. The conclusion of this argument is thus compatible with hardcore essentialism (and both Origin and Category Essentialism).

Third, we accept that Sullivan has presented a puzzle, since it generates several conflicting intuitions. But we also note that Sullivan has picked one of the intuitions to favour, namely, that it's not essential to Ben Franklin that he be alive, and that she has picked the intuition that's weakest and most replaceable. Moreover, when trying to solve this puzzle, we're happy to employ metaphysical considerations rather than purely semantic ones, and see no genuine motivation for relying only on semantic considerations. So we feel free to consider the B-theoretic solution that Sullivan mentions in footnote 9, for example.

Finally, since Sullivan has articulated a genuine puzzle, it's one that she faces as well. But it's hard to see how the anti-essentialist framework that she articulates in her paper solves the puzzle. More specifically, her anti-essentialist framework replaces claims about essential properties with claims about explanatorily relevant characteristics. But, in many contexts, being alive is an explanatorily relevant characteristic of Ben Franklin; how then, in those contexts, will Sullivan solve this puzzle? And in those contexts in which being alive is not explanatorily relevant, what explanatorily relevant characteristics does Franklin have? And is the possession of these features consistent with whatever preferred solution to the puzzle Sullivan accepts?

3.3. The Context-Shift Argument

The final argument we'll discuss is based on the idea that attributions of essential properties are context-sensitive.[11] The phenomenon of context-sensitivity is aptly illustrated by two of the examples she mentions on p. 59:

(1) Gold atom g essentially moves more slowly than a photon. Well, not if special relativity is false.
(2) Peter is essentially an organism. Well, not if he has an immaterial soul.

The worry is that each pair of sentences sounds felicitous but the hardcore essentialist must explain why these four speeches sound felicitous without undermining a major motivation for hardcore essentialism – namely that essential properties can explain our intuitions about reference in other possible worlds.

As we mentioned earlier, we don't endorse hardcore essentialism in order to explain certain semantic intuitions, but rather because there are lots of breakfast foods we simply don't believe we could've been. So we're not exactly the targets of this sort of criticism. We would, however, like to offer our explanation of the appropriateness of speeches denying true essence ascriptions, one that's entirely compatible with hardcore essentialism.

First, let's note that Sullivan's examples have the following form:

(*) P. Well, if Q, then not-P.

Second, note that the second sentence is not the negation of the first. The second sentence is a conditional whose consequent is the negation of the first sentence. If the second sentence were the negation of the first, and speeches of that form seemed felicitous, then we would reasonably suspect that a shift in context produced a change in truth value. But these two sentences are consistent. And so the felicitousness of their joint assertion does not by itself provide a reason to think that a sentence changed truth value: both sentences might be true. It's just that the first sentence is actually true, but it would have been false if certain conditions obtained.

Some instances of the form (*) have antecedents that are metaphysically impossible; we suspect that the one appearing ing (2) might be one as well. Instances of form (*) with necessarily false antencedents are called *counterpossible* conditionals. Counterpossible conditionals raise philosophical issues. On one popular semantics for counterfactuals, a counterfactual conditional of the form *if P were the case, then Q would be case* is true just in case for every possible world in which P&~Q is true, there's a possible world closer to the actual world in which P&Q is true.[12] If a counterfactual has a necessarily false antecedent, this condition is vacuously satisfied, and hence the counterfactual is necessarily true, albeit "vacuously". If this popular semantics is correct, we've a straightforward explanation of why (4) and perhaps (3) sound felicitous: they are both true, albeit each with a vacuously true conditional. But, if counterpossible conditionals can be either false or "non-vacuously" true, this popular semantics for counterfactuals must be revised. Since it's no part of hardcore essentialism that the standard semantics for counterfactual conditionals is correct, we grant here that, e.g., (2) might be (non-vacuously) true.

This worry about context-sensitivity is similar to an argument from Sider (2011: 280-281). Some of Sider's examples have the same form as

Sullivan's and thus don't contain a sentence whose truth-value clearly shifts with context. We think Sider's best examples don't involve conditionals. Here's one:

> I might say: "Johnny can go to the moon (since the technology exists), but not to Mars", whereas later I might say "Johnny can travel to Mars but not to star systems 10,000 light years away (since supraluminal travel violates the laws of nature and humans don't live to be 10,000 years old)."
>
> (Sider 2011: 280)

In this example there's a single sentence – "Johnny can go to Mars" – that's first denied and then asserted. If both utterances are true, then that sentence has different truth values in different contexts. Since this kind of example provides stronger support for contextualism, we reformulate Sullivan's examples as follows:

(1') Gold atom g essentially moves more slowly than a photon. . . . [later, in a context where special relativity's being false is a relevant possibility] Well, g could move more quickly than a photon.

(2') Peter is essentially an organism. . . . [later, in a context where the falsity of physicalism is a relevant possibility] Well, he could fail to be a organism.

We'll focus on explaining why these speeches sound felicitous since we take this to be a harder challenge for the hardcore essentialist.

Note that Sullivan and Sider's examples are all about *de re* necessity. But the phenomenon that Sullivan and Sider drawn attention to is not restricted to *de re* necessity. There are similar examples involving *de dicto* necessity:

(1") Necessarily, nothing moves faster than light. . . . [later, in a context where special relativity's being false is a relevant possibility] Well, possibly a thing travels faster than light.

(2") Necessarily, human persons are organisms. . . . [later, in a context where the falsity of physicalism is a relevant possibility] Well, possibly human persons are non-organisms.

The general issue is that *modal* language is context-sensitive. The issue is not specific to *de re* modal language. We don't think that the context-sensitivity of modal language by itself provides a reason to think that there's no such thing as absolute (metaphysical) necessity. We think that there's a worry for hardcore essentialism only if the context-sensitivity of modal talk cannot be fruitfully explained without abandoning hardcore essentialism. We believe that this is not so.

We prefer an explanation of this context-sensitivity that appeals to restrictions on the domain of possible worlds. We accept the standard connection between being possibly true and being true at some possible world; varieties of possibility and necessity are to be understood in terms of being true at some or all possible worlds of a certain sort. *Metaphysically* necessary propositions, whether they are *de dicto* or *de re*, are those that are true at every possible world. But rarely is this strictest kind of necessity invoked in contexts in which one says, "this had to be the case" or "it has to be this way". Typically, some weaker kind of necessity is invoked, and with it a correspondingly stronger kind of possibility. For example, consider the sentence, "It's impossible for something to move faster than the speed of light".[13] We think utterances of this sentence are (probably) often true.[14] Perhaps they are uttered in contexts in which the relevant kind of necessity invoked is *nomological*: nomologically necessary propositions are those that are true at every metaphysically possible world where all of our laws of nature hold. If so, in those contexts, "nothing can move faster than the speed of light" expresses a truth even if there are some possible worlds in which things move faster than the speed of light.

A similar story can be told about the *de re* sentence, "gold atom g essentially moves slower than the speed of light". It's a familiar fact that we don't always talk about all that there is, even when we use the word "all" – as witnessed by the famous sentence "all the beer is in the fridge".[15] We grant that typical utterances of "gold atom g essentially moves slower than the speed of light" are true, provided that "essentially" in this sentence means "at all possible worlds" and that this "all" can be contextually restricted, rather than "at absolutely all possible worlds", which contains an expression designed to prevent "all" from being restricted. Typical uses of "gold atom g essentially moves slower than the speed of light" are uttered in contexts in which only some but not all possible worlds are relevant. But the truth expressed in these contexts is compatible with the truth (if it's a truth) that there are possible worlds in which gold atom g moves faster than the speed of light.

Hardcore essentialism does not imply that modal talk is not context-sensitive.[16] Hardcore essentialism does not deny that there are ordinary uses of "essential" that are context-sensitive, though we personally are suspicious that these uses are very common; talk of how something must be or can be, however, is very common. That said, we'd prefer to reserve "essential property" as a technical expression synonymous for "property had at absolutely all worlds (in which its bearer exists)".

In general, shifts in contexts are often correlated with shifts in the domain of quantification. Still, though, there's an unrestricted domain containing all the possible worlds. A proposition is (absolutely and without qualification) necessary when it's true in every possible world. An object has a property (absolutely and without qualification) essentially when it has the property in every possible world where it exists.

This explanation of the context-sensitivity of modal language (both *de dicto* and *de re*) is entirely compatible with hardcore essentialism. It only goes so far though. So far we've explained only the context-shift in speech 1'. However, speech 2' requires a different treatment. Let's assume for the argument's sake that human persons are essentially organisms. Speech 2' says that Peter could've failed to be an organism. That claim is false as long as we're quantifying over all the possible worlds or some restricted set of them – there's no possible world where Peter isn't an organism.

One option for us is just to say that speech 2' is not entirely true, since it includes a false claim. Sullivan might ask: if it is false, why does it sound felicitous? But we don't think that speeches 2' sounds felicitous; it sounds to us rather bad. Speech 2 does sound felicitous. But we feel no temptation to conflate 2 and 2', and we've already argued that the felicity of 2 poses no special problem for the hardcore essentialist.

But there's a second option for the hardcore essentialist that's more concessive. On this second option, speech 2' is true. But not because the second sentence is true when "could" is understood as "metaphysically possible". Rather, on the second option, the second sentence of this speeches is best interpreted as expressing *epistemic* possibility. Moreover, they sound felicitous only when interpreted this way. An epistemic possibility is a situation that we cannot rule out. Sometimes we cannot rule out things that cannot really happen. So some propositions are epistemically possible but not metaphysically possible. Speech 2' plausibly contains an examples of this phenomenon: if our evidence leaves us uncertain whether Peter absolutely must be an organism, we cannot decisively say it is true; and it's in this sense (and this sense only) that it *might* be false.[17]

We agree with Sullivan that the truth-value of sentences that say of some given objects that they must be such-and-such ways can vary across contexts (because, in general, sentences with modal vocabulary are context-sensitive). We also agree with Sullivan that what we're trying to explain in a given context can also play a role in determining the domain of possible worlds that in turn determine the truth-conditions for the modal vocabulary uttered in that context. For example, when we're interested in giving causal explanations, we typically restrict our attention to the nomologically possible worlds. But often further restrictions are in play. Consider the sentence "Sam is essentially earthbound".[18] This sentence is true in contexts in which the only worlds invoked are those nomologically possible worlds in which Sam does not leave Earth. In general, those properties that Sullivan calls "explanatorily crucial properties" often play an important role: in many contexts, a possible world is within the domain of quantification only if objects within it instantiate those properties that are explanatorily crucial in that context. In short, what we're interested in explaining can help shape the truth-conditions for sentences employing modal expressions in the context of explanation, and we view this as a very important insight captured by Sullivan's positive proposal. We'll have more to say about Sullivan's views on explanatorily crucial properties in the next section.

4. Explanation-Relative Essentialism

After she argues against hardcore essentialism, Sullivan considers what we should say instead about ascriptions of essential features. She rejects what she calls *pure anti-essentialism*, the view that *de re* modal claims are unintelligible. She seems to agree with the hardcore essentialist that some objects must have some properties, but she thinks that the 'must' is *relative to some parameter*, rather than absolute and without qualification. She endorses *relative essentialism*, the thesis that there's at least one object and qualitative and discriminating property such that the object must (relative to some parameter) have the property if it exists.

Next Sullivan searches for the appropriate parameter. She proposes *explanation-relative essentialism*, which claims that the relevant parameter is an explanatory framework. Here's her official statement of explanation-relative essentialism:

> An object o is essentially P relative to framework E iff: (i) o has P; (ii) in any good explanation of type E which involves o, o has P; and (iii) there are objective norms governing explanations of type E.

Here Sullivan identifies the essential properties (relative to a norm-governed framework) with the explanatorily crucial properties. Interpreted uncharitably, explanation-relative essentialism changes the subject. The explanatorily crucial properties are essential only in the sense that facts about an object cannot be explaining without mentioning those properties. This is not the sense of 'essential' that has been traditionally discussed in philosophy. In that sense, a property is essential to an object when the object cannot exist without having the property.

Are these two senses of 'essential' coextensive? Perhaps a thing cannot (relative to a norm-governed framework) exist without a property if and only if that property must (relative to that framework) be mentioned in any good explanation involving that object. Both directions of this biconditional strike us as implausible.

Suppose we're interested in explaining why students get the grades they do, and in particular why Jasmine has a 4.0 GPA. It turns out that Jasmine studies very hard, and in this context, any explanation of her 4.0 GPA must mention that she studies very hard. But even relative to the framework of grade explanations, Jasmine could stop studying so hard for any number of reasons, and she wouldn't thereby cease to exist. Jasmine has a property that's explanatorily crucial in this framework, but that she could nonetheless exist without.

There are also some properties that play no crucial explanatory role, which we nonetheless cannot exist without. Everyone reading this has the property of being a non-poached-egg essentially, since none of you could've been a poached egg. But it's very hard to think of a norm-governed explanatory framework in which *every* good explanation involving one of us cites the property of being a non-poached-egg. Our non-poached-egged-ness is entirely explanatorily irrelevant in most contexts. Even when the property of being a non-poached-egg is explanatorily relevant, it's never explanatorily crucial. Thus, there's a property that we cannot exist without, even though that property plays no crucial explanatory role. This is an unsurprising result from our perspective, since we did not posit essential properties because of the explanatory role they play.

Sullivan (this volume) claims that explanation-relative essentialism can explain why certain kinds of context-shifts are appropriate and others are not. According to her, speeches (1)–(2), which we discussed in the previous section, are felicitous because they involve acceptable shifts between explanatory frameworks.

We also suspect that explanation-relative essentialism is compatible with hardcore essentialism. Explanation-relative essentialism says that some objects have some properties essentially *relative to an explanatory framework*, rather than absolutely and without qualification. But Sullivan admits that 'it may be the case that some objects must have some properties in *every* explanatory context with objective norms' (58). She calls such properties *super-essential*. We think that a super-essential property would be worth calling *absolutely and unqualifiedly essential*. If that's right, explanation-relative essentialism is compatible with hardcore essentialism.

Sullivan claims that there are three differences between her view and her opponent's:

First, harder-core essentialists typically assume that facts about essences are needed to ground explanatory norms. The explanation-relative essentialist thinks facts about explanatory norms are prior. . . . Second, the harder-core essentialists assume there is only one privileged context of explanation—the metaphysical context—which determines absolute essence ascriptions. The explanation-relative essentialist thinks the metaphysical context is (at best) one among many. . . . Third, while the harder-core essentialist may think there is a single, exhaustive essential/accidental classification of an object's properties, the explanation-relative essentialist thinks that, outside of a context of explanation, such a classification is incoherent.

(58–59)

At best, these are differences between explanation-relative essentialism and *harder*-core essentialism. Harder-core essentialism is the conjunction of hardcore essentialism and the claim that essential properties are parts of the *real natures* of objects. We're only defending hardcore essentialism, not harder-core essentialism.

At worst, there are only differences between explanation-relative essentialism and things that 'harder-core essentialists typically assume' or 'may think'. We don't think harder-core essentialism *entails* that facts about essences ground explanatory norms, or that there's only one privileged context of explanation, or that there's a single, exhaustive essential/accidental distinction. So it seems to us that even harder-core essentialism is compatible with explanation-relative essentialism.

To sum up: we believe that Sullivan has presented several interesting challenges to hardcore essentialism, but at the end of the day, these challenges have been met. Are there essential properties? We answer, 'yes'.

Notes

1. Here are three qualms about her formulation of hardcore essentialism. First: hardcore essentialism as she formulates it is committed to properties, but this seems inessential to the view itself. And, even if we accept some properties, we might not accept negative properties. But we're confident that we're essentially not poached eggs. Second qualm: her account of qualitative properties as those properties for which it's possible that more than one thing can instantiate it seems incorrect, since this account incorrectly classifies disjunctions of non-qualitative properties as being qualitative. Consider, for example, the property of being either Kris McDaniel or Steve Steward, or being a student of Phil Bricker; the latter property is not straightforwardly disjunctive, but it's also misclassified. Third qualm: a background assumption Sullivan makes is that existence is 'univocal', but one of us denies this: see McDaniel (2009, 2013) for defenses of modes and degrees of being, respectively. Given modes or degrees of being, a more subtle account of essential properties might be apt.
2. Although Lewis (1986) does not speak in terms of fundamental facts, it would be natural to see view two as a consequence of his modal realism. (Note that modal realism is compatible with hardcore essentialism; see McDaniel [2004, 2006] for versions of modal realism that incorporate hardcore essentialism.)
3. Compare with Cameron (2009) and Sider (2003).
4. Strictly speaking, the hardcore essentialist is only committed to the claim that there's some thing and some property that this thing absolutely must have if it exists. Even if, contrary to fact, we could be breakfast foods, hardcore essentialism would still be true if we absolutely couldn't be numbers, or numbers couldn't be tropes, or tropes couldn't be regions of space, or regions of space couldn't be events.
5. Lewis (1986) defends both perdurantism and absolutely unrestricted composition.
6. We can say similar things on some non-perdurantist views; see, e.g., Steen (2010).
7. Olson (2004) discusses both disjuncts.

8. Kripke (1980) famously argues for origin essentialism.
9. Category essentialism is one variety of *sortal essentialism*, defended by Wiggins (1980). We are not aware of many discussions of category essentialism. Penelope Mackie, a devoted critic of essential properties, admits that broad categories such as *number* and *event* might be essential (Mackie 2006: 166).
10. There are two potential complications. What if *past object* and *present object* are ontological categories? Note that in this, story, Battra doesn't change from being present to being past, but at some point in the future it would. What if *actual object* and *merely possible object* are ontological categories? Then anything that exists in the actual world and in another possible world would fail to belong to all its ontological categories essentially. Both of us take at least one of these possibilities seriously; see McDaniel (forthcoming, chapters 3, 4, and 9) for discussion of whether *past object, present object, possible object,* and *actual object* are ontological categories.
11. We thank Meghan Sullivan for suggesting this argument to us.
12. A classic text on counterfactuals is Lewis (1973).
13. See, e.g., Lewis (1973: ch 1).
14. We don't really want to go out on a limb here with respect to physics or its philosophy; this sentence is offered merely as an aid to illuminate the phenomenon we're discussing.
15. We do not know when this sentence first entered the philosophical literature; but see Lewis (1986: 3) for one place.
16. The "harder-core essentialist" who believes in real natures – such as Fine (1994) and Lowe (2008) among others – might deny any context sensitivity to attributions of real natures to things. But we do not think any of Sullivan's sentences are plausibly read as ascribing real natures to the things in question, and our focus is on *de re* modality throughout.
17. In personal communication, Sullivan notes that these speeches might be read as invoking epistemic possibility, and grants that this would provide the hardcore essentialist with an explanation of the felicitousness of these speeches. But she also worries that going this route won't vindicate the semantic motivation for hardcore essentialism. Perhaps this interpretation doesn't vindicate the semantic motivation for hardcore essentialism; we're indifferent to whether it does, but also not sure she is correct. We believe that not all uses of "could" or "might" in ordinary contexts must express metaphysical possibility or some restriction thereof rather than epistemic possibility. And we still think some intuitions can guide our theorizing – the ones that retain their force after critical reflection. We just don't think the alleged intuition that "could" as used in speech 2' expresses metaphysical possibility retains its force once we see the difference between epistemic and metaphysical possibility.
18. We owe this example to Sullivan.

References

Cameron, Ross. 2009. "What's Metaphysical about Metaphysical Necessity?" *Philosophy and Phenomenological Research* 79 (1): 1–16.
Fine, Kit. 1994. "Essence and Modality." *Philosophical Perspectives* 8: 1–16.
Goddu, G.C. 2003. "Time Travel and Changing the Past: (Or How to Kill Yourself and Live to Tell the Tale)." *Ratio* 16: 16–32.
Hudson, Hud and Ryan Wasserman. 2010. "Van Inwagen on Time Travel and Changing the Past." Co-authored with H. Hudson. In D. Zimmerman (ed.), *Oxford Studies in Metaphysics* 5: 41–49. Oxford: Oxford University Press.
Kripke, Saul. 1980. *Naming and Necessity.* Blackwell Publishing: Cambridge, MA.
Lewis, David. 1973. *Counterfactuals.* Blackwell Publishing.
———. 1976. "The Paradoxes of Time Travel." *American Philosophical Quarterly* 13: 145–152.
———. 1986. *On the Plurality of Worlds.* Blackwell Publishing.

Lowe, E.J. 2008. "Two Notions of Being: Entity and Essence". In Robin Le Poidevin (ed.), *Being: Developments of Contemporary Metaphysics, Royal Institute of Philosophy Supplement*, volume 62, 23–48.

Mackie, Penelope. 2006. *How Things Might Have Been*. Clarendon Press.

McDaniel, Kris. 2003. "Modal Realism with Overlap." *Australasian Journal of Philosophy* 82 (1): 137–152.

———. 2006. "Modal Realisms." *Philosophical Perspectives: Metaphysics* 20: 303–331.

———. 2009. "Ways of Being". In David Chalmers, David Manley, and Ryan Wasserman (eds.), *Metametaphysics: New Essays on the Foundations of Ontology*. Oxford: Oxford University Press.

———. 2013. "Degrees of Being." *Philosophers' Imprint* 13 (19): 1–19.

———. Forthcoming. *The Fragmentation of Being*.

Olson, Eric. 2004. "Animalism and the Corpse Problem." *Australasian Journal of Philosophy* 82 (2): 265–274.

Sider, Theodore. 2003. "Reductive Theories of Modality". In Michael Loux and Dean Zimmerman (eds.), *The Oxford Handbook of Metaphysics*. Oxford: Oxford University Press.

———. 2011. *Writing the Book of the World*. Oxford: Oxford University Press.

Steen, Irem Kurtsal. 2010. "Three-Dimensionalist's Semantic Solution to Diachronic Vagueness." *Philosophical Studies* 150 (1): 79–96.

van Inwagen, Peter. 2009. "Changing the Past." *Oxford Studies in Metaphysics* 5: 3–28.

Wiggins, David. 1980. *Sameness and Substance*. Blackwell Publishing.

PART III

Are There Any Worldly States of Affairs?

CHAPTER 5

Does the World Contain States of Affairs? Yes

DANIEL NOLAN

We appear to talk about states of entities and of systems all of the time. Talk of states is commonplace in ordinary talk about the world: we naturally talk about the state of our clothes, or the state of the economy, or the state of the floor in a child's bedroom. Almost any area of inquiry helps itself to talk of states. Computer programming is all about how to ensure that computers in one state transition into another. A major part of chemistry seems to concern how one state of a system leads to another via a series of chemical reactions. Psychology would be transformed if we refused to believe in psychological states. Economists are asked to comment on the state of the economy, or sections of the economy. And so on.

Despite the fact that this talk is everywhere, in everyday talk and in many areas of inquiry, there is some temptation to be suspicious of taking it at face value. It is an appealing thought to some that while the world may contain coffee cups and tables, it does not contain in addition a *state* of a particular coffee cup being on a particular table. Perhaps this state talk is best understood as indirect talk about, for example, coffee cups and tables, and only apparently about another kind of entity, a state? Or perhaps it is indirect talk not just about coffee cups and the like, but also about properties and relations of entities such as coffee cups? Or despite appearances, is it all a mistake?

In this chapter, I argue we should resist that temptation, and recognise states as real parts of the world just as much as 'things' such as coffee cups and properties such as shapes are. Entities such as these are sometimes called 'facts', and sometimes 'states of affairs'. Calling them 'facts' in particular is a contested usage, since that expression also gets used for true propositions. It seems to me that 'states of affairs' is the least misleading general expression for the kind of beings I am arguing for here: the word 'state' suggests the question 'state of what', while some states are not obviously states of any single thing. (The state of the coffee cup being on the table is a state that involves two things, but is it a state of a single thing, e.g. a cup-table *system*, or perhaps a whole of which the cup and table are parts? Maybe, but systems and cup-table aggregates are more controversial entities than cups or tables: and particular *systems* rather look like states of affairs themselves.) 'State of affairs' has the advantage that 'affairs' looks like a rather non-specific noun and has at least the tendency to defuse the question of *which* entity (or entities) a state is 'of'. Despite 'state of affairs' being perhaps the best term for the kind of entity I am concerned with, in this chapter, I will normally just talk of 'states' for brevity.

In some philosophical projects, 'state' and 'state of affairs' are used to tag quite specific kinds of postulated entities. Here, I am using the expressions a little more broadly: so situations, circumstances, scenarios, and other such entities are all things I am happy to count as states of affairs. At least, that is, if we think that they are found in the world rather than being mental entities or non-spatio-temporal entities that only have some sort of representational relation to the world: if a scenario is merely a kind of mental content or description of entities in the world, they would not be states in the sense I am trying to convey.

The main style of argument in this paper for recognition of states as genuine entities will be by pointing out how states seem to play an important explanatory role in theories that are both successful, and which we already accept. One way such arguments work is to appeal to pre-existing beliefs of an audience: if you think theory X is basically correct, and theory X implies that there are states, then a commitment you already have provides you with a reason to believe there are states. Another way is through an 'inference to the best explanation': whether or not you initially accept theory X, if you become convinced that theory X is a good theory of something, and it implies that there are states, that gives you reason to adopt theory X, and the belief that there are states. Provided, at least, that the theory is 'good' in the right sort of way. (I'll leave aside the interesting question what 'inference to the best explanation' has to do with *explanation*, if anything. The expression 'inference to the best explanation' has a life of its own, at this point.)

Both kinds of argument can be resisted. Pointing out that things you already believe imply something should sometimes lead you to revise the things you initially believed, rather than just take on the implied commitment. A theory can be apparently good, but only apparently, or have an equally good or better rival: if X is a good theory of something that implies that there are states, but we notice that Y is a better theory of that thing but does not imply that there are states, then choosing X and belief in states no longer seems a sensible response to the fact that X is a good theory. However, almost every philosophical argument can be resisted by someone with sufficient motivation: the point is not to force acceptance, but to make a sufficiently appealing case that a theory seems preferable to the alternatives. (Or at least that's my aim, here.)

1. States, Events, and Tropes

To help get clear on what I am defending, and to lay some building blocks for the defence, it will be useful to compare states to some other supposed entities discussed in metaphysics. Consider events. Talk about events seems even more ubiquitous than talk of states. Matches lighting, games of football, plane flights, walks in the park, and so on: and again, talking about events is not just part of our common-sense ways of describing the world, but is ubiquitous in science and other areas of inquiry. (Imagine history without mention of any historical events, for example! No battles, elections, coronations, mysterious deaths. . .or any changes at all.)

Some of our talk about events concerns *general* events: events that occur over and over, such as the morning sunrise or the Olympic Games. I will focus, for the moment, on *particular* events, such as the sunrise this very morning, or the 2000 Olympic Games. It is possible to deny the existence of particular events, perhaps by trying to reconstruct our apparent commitment to them entirely in terms of things and perhaps their properties. But on the face of it, that project looks quixotic. Why even be tempted to deny that there are long walks on the beach or particular screenings of movies, or performances of songs? Perhaps we could capture much of what we believe about the world by talking only of people walking on beaches and never of the walks they take; or of theatres showing movies but no movie-showings. But finding a way to cast a theory of the world that never commits to events can look more like a pathological search for euphemism than hard-headed austerity.

The way some people think about events, events essentially involve *changes*: the death of a monarch is an event, but a continuation of a reign is less obviously an event. An event may not involve much change—very slow motion may constitute an event, and a steel bucket rusting away may be one drawn-out event, even if not very much happens in any ten-minute period of that event. I am not sure our ordinary word 'event' is so limited: it does not seem to be a stretch to talk about static setups as involving boring events, and even a non-occurrence can sometimes be described as an event. (A dog not barking, for example.) Nevertheless, let us suppose, for the time being, that events only occur when there are changes. Some theorists want to distinguish *events* from *processes*—and while there are sometimes reasons to distinguish processes from other things, I am using the term 'event' generously enough to cover both here. (So, for example, a given baking of a cake is an event in my sense, even if it is interrupted before a cake is produced.)

Events are apparently different entities from the objects that feature in them or the properties and relations those objects have: the event of writing a letter is different both from the letter produced, and the properties of the letter such as being five paragraphs in length. In the next section, I will argue that our recognition of the existence of events gives us a reason to recognise states too, but some analogies should already be clear.

Another variety of entity that is sometimes postulated are *property instances*, or as they are sometimes called, *tropes*. These are the particular features things have, as opposed to the general features that are shared. The blue of *my* shirt, that can fade or be dyed away, as opposed to that general shade of blue, that will still be found elsewhere no matter what happens to my shirt. We often talk about the properties and relations of people as if they are specific—my anger can fade without anger itself disappearing from the world, and the particular relation I stand in to each of my brothers came into existence only a few decades ago, even though brotherhood in general has been around much longer. Typical property instances seem different both from entities like my shirt or my brother, and also different from general properties and relations, though tropes do seem to be found in the world—we talk of *seeing* the shade of my shirt, for example, which would be difficult if it were not to be found where my shirt is. The existence of property instances is a little more controversial than the existence of events, but those who already believe in them should be predisposed to think that there are entities to be found in our world other than things such as shirts and general properties such as a particular shade of blue.

2. Arguments for the Existence of States

One kind of argument for the existence of states takes advantage of the connections between states, on the one hand, and events and tropes, on the other. Given how I have characterised states of affairs, both events and tropes look like good candidates to be examples of states. It is natural to see events as a special kind of state—the kind that involves a change. Or to put it the other way around, it is natural to see the changes as a special case of a more general class of circumstances or scenarios—and that more general class is naturally identified as the states of affairs. Likewise, tropes occur when particular objects stand in properties or relations—and an object's having a property (e.g. a stovetop's being hot or an economy's being in recession) looks like an excellent candidate to be a state of affairs in the sense introduced. Many people already believe that events exist (I suspect it is only philosophers, and perhaps some bored teenagers, who think that nothing ever happens). Anyone who has seen the blueness of their favourite shirt fade in the wash might be inclined to think that there is such an entity as the blueness of the shirt, distinct from the general property of blue which the shirt had and then lost, but which never faded, and so, if particularised properties are just states, might also be inclined to be convinced that their shirt was in one state, and is now in another. My own view is that both events and tropes should be counted as states, and we get a pleasing unification of a disparate bunch of entities if we think that there is a general category that is talked about in different ways. So in this way our recognition of, for example, events should lead us to recognise the existence of states of affairs.

An even more straightforward argument than the argument just presented from events, property instances, and the rest, is an argument that was implicit in my opening remarks. Beliefs we already have seem to imply that there are states: you can open the newspaper for information about the state of the economy, most competent cooks can update you about the state of a cake mix they are preparing, an engineer inspecting an old bridge can authoritatively report on the state of that bridge, and so on. Many of these beliefs are ones we take to be very well supported by our evidence about the world and by legitimate expertise: an engineer making predictions about a bridge, for example, has a long tradition of careful observation and experiment behind her, and humans have got pretty good at our theory of bridges over the years. (You might have noticed we can build large and elaborate bridges, and most bridges that are built well according to engineering standards stay up pretty reliably.)

If we believe a theory that implies that there are states, and we have excellent reasons for believing that theory, then we should conclude that there are states. And when we have many excellent theories in different areas all telling us that there are states, the case is even stronger. Seen in this light, disbelieving in states can seem like disbelieving in cakes or bridges: there *are* potential philosophical positions that reject the existence of such things, but we would want to see a pretty spectacular argument before we should be persuaded.

As well as these apparently commonplace encounters with states of affairs, many successful scientific inquiries focus a lot of attention on entities that, on examination, appear to be states. Trying to do psychology while ignoring mental states is very difficult. Economists concern themselves with predicting and explaining economic circumstances: and the economy itself is plausibly understood as a large and complex state in which we collectively find ourselves. (Talk of economic 'conditions' is more common than talk of economic states: but when talking about particular conditions, as opposed to general types of conditions, I think 'condition' talk is naturally interpreted as being about states of affairs in the sense I am employing here.)

States even appear in what seem to be our most fundamental scientific inquiries. Pictures of the world drawn from physics suggest that the entire natural world is nothing but a collection of states of matter and energy (or perhaps matter and energy *plus* the states they are in). Quantum mechanics is up to its neck in talk of states and systems: the fundamental target of theorising often looks to be the attempt to properly describe the evolution of a state-space (where a state-space is, at least at first blush, the mathematical description of a complex state, or perhaps a collection of states). If all these theories apparently about states and systems have excellent powers to predict the outcomes of very precise experiments and enable the construction of new and powerful apparatuses, that strongly suggests these theories are on to something. Since these theories are best understood as being about states, that should make us confident that the states they describe exist (or perhaps states somewhat like the ones they describe, if we think our current theories are probably still wrong about some of the details).

Those who are suspicious of states of affairs are typically not sceptics across the board, and typically do not reject either common-sense entities such as cakes or bridges, nor scientific entities such as minds or economies (unless those themselves are states), nor subatomic particles, objects with mass, and so on. Nor do they reject wholesale the expertise of cooks or bridge builders, or economists or psychologists, or chemists and physicists. In response to the argument just outlined, they are likely to say one of two things. They are likely either to say that ordinary 'state' talk does not imply that states exist or that the world contains states of affairs, or alternatively that while existing beliefs and theories would, if true, require there to be states of affairs, there are close rival theories that would perform just as well for prediction and understanding, but lack this commitment to states of affairs.

Either response to these arguments from common sense and science will agree that there is something importantly right about a lot of ordinary state talk. So those who reject the existence of states will reject the charge that they should be lumped in with wholesale sceptics about our ability to get much about the world right, either through everyday evidence gathering such as reading a newspaper or keeping an eye on some cake mix, or through more specialised scientific means.

The two possible responses to the widespread use of state talk in well-confirmed theories deserve separate treatment. I will call the first response, that sentences apparently talking of states do not really require states of affairs, a 'linguistic' response, since it relies on a hypothesis about the functioning of certain parts of language. The second response, that our theories do tell us there are states of affairs but they are wrong about that, I will call the 'revisionary' response, since the truth would require revision. (Though some who favour this response may think that outside philosophy we should carry on as we have been—perhaps an untrue theory committed to states might have some worthwhile advantages the true theories would lack, for example.)

My response to the linguistic response will be the focus of the next section of this paper. Before turning to arguments about the language of states, however, it is worth saying something briefly about the revisionary response. What is wrong with holding that our ordinary talk about states is false?

There are many forms a revisionary response might take. But a common structure will include a suggestion of what form the truth in the area might take, either in detail or at least a sketch of the kind of thing; together with some reasons to think that the alternative, so described, will be adequate for our theoretical purposes—and ideally some motivations to prefer the revisionary alternative. Arguments against specific revisionary responses will often depend on the details of how this structure is filled in, of course. But there are a few general suspicions that any revisionary suggestion will face. One is whether they can adequately specify the candidate to be the literal truth in the area of our talk about states. Such a specification would preferably be systematic—if they can only gesture at an alternative in a few specific cases, that should not give us much confidence that alternatives to theories postulating states will be appealing across the board. And it should be adequate for all, or most, of the purposes that we invoked states for in the first place. It remains to be seen whether either of these desired features for an alternative can be achieved.

Suppose, however, we get to the stage where a well-worked-out alternative to theories committed to states has been presented to us, or at least adequately gestured towards, by a revisionist, and we become convinced, by one means or another, that the alternative is adequate to the purposes for which we had our original beliefs and theories about states. There would still be one more objection to face. The fact is that the theories and beliefs that *have* succeeded up until now are those that tell us there are states of affairs. (This, at least, is not in dispute between me and the revisionists as I have characterised them.) In general, I think, the theories that have an *actual* track record of success and a history of surviving testing should be preferred to theories that are in other respects equally good (e.g. they both accommodate the evidence so far) but which have not yet passed the test of being actually relied upon and tested. Even if some systematic theory that did not postulate states can be cooked up by a sufficiently ingenious philosopher that manages to accommodate our predictions and explanations so far, we would want to see some additional advantages to it before switching.

This methodological principle is not uncontroversial: though one reason I think it is plausible is that it is often possible to cook up rival explanatory schemes for evidence we have but disagree with our current opinions in some respects: and if they had to be taken equally seriously, we run the risk that we will have to give up nearly all of our beliefs one by one, due to the availability of alternative theories that reject those particular beliefs but do rather well at predicting and explaining our evidence. This seems to me particularly true when we are choosing between philosophical theories: a theory in which tables are just Ideas in the mind of God might predict and explain our course of experience with tables fairly well, but even if I were convinced that it did okay at matching my current predictions and explanations, that would not incline me to even suspend judgement about whether tables are non-mental entities in a physical world.

Preferring the commitments of our actually successful theories until an alternative can be shown not just to be a rival but an improvement should not be so important a force to lead to stagnation. Revolutions in our ways of thinking are possible: the germ theory of disease overturned a lot of common-sense beliefs and medical doctrines, but it should have been accepted (about many diseases) even despite this. Revisionists who accept that their candidate for the truth should be an *improvement* on our current state-laden theories may still wish to make that case. So debate with revisionists will no doubt continue: but at the moment I think revisionists still face heavy theoretical burdens that they need to do more to discharge.

3. Understanding State Talk

Let us then move from considering the revisionist to considering the 'linguistic response' to the apparent ubiquity of states of affairs posited by successful and well-tested theories. This response does not ask us to revise our commitment to theories that apparently postulate states: it is *true* that, for example, a certain politician was surprised in a state of undress, or that the economy is in a better state now than it was in 2009. It is just that we misunderstand these claims if we think they are telling us that there are a special kind of entity, states of affairs (of clothing arrangement in the first case, of economic activity or of economic actors in the second). Instead, this talk is about nothing more than politicians and clothing, economic actors and perhaps their activities, and so on. Somehow, talk apparently about states is really only about entities other than states of affairs: and so even if the claims are true, and we genuinely believe them, it would be a mistake to infer from them that there are the states of affairs they apparently describe.

The linguistic response and the revisionary response can sometimes resemble each other closely: one way to construct a revisionary alternative is to offer a mapping from state talk to sentences that apparently do not talk about states, and the most standard way to flesh out a linguistic response is to provide a systematic map from sentences apparently about states to sentences that are apparently not. Some opponents of states of affairs are not even clear which they intend—merely telling us that they think state talk can be 'paraphrased away' without being clear about the status of the paraphrase.

I should distinguish the linguistic response from another kind of response, which is gaining in popularity and can be seen as hostile to states of affairs even though, in my view, it falls neither into the revisionary or linguistic camps. This is the view that while sentences apparently about states of affairs are true, and are indeed about states of affairs (contra the linguistic response), there are not states of affairs *in reality*, or states of affairs are not *truthmakers* for claims about states, or that states of affairs are not *fundamental*. While I am personally tempted by the view that some states of affairs are indeed fundamental, my task today is to argue that states of affairs exist—once that is conceded, we can have a further debate about how metaphysically deep this discovery is.

There are many ways the linguistic response could be developed, and different versions will look quite different depending in part on the resources they rely upon. An attempt to account for state talk just in terms of ordinary physical objects will look quite different from one that leans heavily on invoking general properties or abstract propositions, for example, or which invokes events but argues that events should not be seen as a kind of state. There is a lot of scope for technical virtuosity in developing these linguistic analyses, and subtle issues can arise in the details. I am glad that people pursue this sort of project from time to time, since it helps us understand the dizzying range of alternatives we potentially have available for systematically accounting for how our talk is connected to reality. However, even without going into the details, a number of serious concerns can be raised for any linguistic response: just as with the revisionary response, I think these options have a steep uphill battle ahead.

The first is that there is a cost in initial plausibility: the surface of these sentences suggests strongly they are about states, as competent speakers, we are initially inclined to judge they are about states, and a linguistic theory that denies they are about states and holds that competent users are systematically mistaken about what they are talking about has the appearances against it. This can be overcome with good enough evidence, of course, and some of the most impressive human intellectual achievements consist in establishing a theory that the initial appearances are against. But in general, overturning the apparently secure judgements of competent judges requires some impressive reasons.

Second, it has proved very difficult, in this area and others, to offer systematic paraphrases that seem adequate but avoid talk about suspect entities. Some of these difficulties are due to how pervasive and complex state talk can be. Simple sentences such as, 'John was in an agitated state' might just amount to something such as, 'John was agitated'. But we do not just talk about states in simple sentences such as this. We compare one state with another; we quantify over states, saying all X states are Y states or that there are some Z states; we talk about relationships between different states; and, in complex enough sentences, we do all of these things at once. Trying to account for our talk about states while treating it as really talk about something else looks, on the face of it, as difficult as trying to account for our mathematical language while treating it as being about something other than numbers, sets, functions, and other mathematical objects. Once the hurdles to systematically understanding state language as really being about something else are appreciated, it looks more and more tempting to think that state talk is what it appears to be at first glance: talk about states of affairs.

It may be that a suitably clever scheme can be constructed so that we can adequately capture what state language is doing in other terms. But until more progress is made on these projects, they have a bit of the air of projects designed to understand physical object language as being about something other than physical objects (e.g. the old projects of understanding apparent talk about external objects as talk about sense data). Maybe something along those lines could be achieved, but the prospects do not look bright that it will lead us to reject the face-value reading of either talk about physical objects, in the sense data case, or talk about states, in the current case.

4. Conclusion

One reaction to metaphysical arguments such as this is to dismiss the problems engaged with as uninteresting or unimportant, so in conclusion I should say something about why I think this dispute is worth having. I suspect there are many good answers to the question of why this issue is interesting: after all, different people are interested in different things, so the reason something is interesting to one person might be different to why it is interesting to another. One is the intrinsic interest—whether there are states of affairs in the world we experience and theorise about is not obvious, and the self-conscious realisation that states exist is as wide-ranging and as informative as the discovery of ordinary objects or of properties. If we came across people with a strange intellectual tradition or cognitive disorder that meant that it had never dawned on them that there were physical objects, those of them who care about understanding the world would appreciate having this aspect of the world revealed to them. The realisation that states of affairs are real features of our world seems to me of the same order of interest and excitement.

As well as the intrinsic interest of states of affairs, recognition of their reality holds out a lot of promise in philosophy. To name just three metaphysical projects where states of affairs have been thought to be helpful, (i) they are invoked to unify our understanding of different causal relationships (see Menzies's 1989 use of 'real situations'), (ii) they are invoked to explain how objects have properties and what in the world corresponds to our true claims (Armstrong 1997), and (iii) appeal to unobtaining states of affairs is one way to try to make sense of our talk of mere possibilities (see, for instance, Plantinga 1976). But a more widespread appreciation of the centrality of states of affairs would shift some of the focus, not just in metaphysics, but in philosophy of representation (both in mind and language), philosophy of science, epistemology, and potentially beyond (there is relatively little discussion of the role of states of affairs in the aesthetics literature, for example, especially outside the metaphysics of aesthetics and art). Understanding better the relationships between states, and between states and other entities, may be the key to unlocking understanding of a lot of the world we find ourselves in. Recognition that states are to be taken seriously is one of the first steps in this process.

References

Armstrong, D.M. 1997. *A World of States of Affairs*. Cambridge: Cambridge University Press.
Menzies, P. 1989. "A Unified Account of Causal Relata." *Australasian Journal of Philosophy* 67 (1): 59–83.
Plantinga, A. 1976. "Actualism and Possible Worlds." *Theoria* 42: 139–160.

CHAPTER 6

Does the World Contain States of Affairs? No

JOSEPH MELIA

1. Introduction

If anything deserves to be called a tenet of common sense, it is the view that concrete particulars exist. Tables, chairs and desks are familiar, mundane and unmysterious. We see them, rearrange them, interact with them, bump into them and spill our coffee over them.[1] Concrete particulars are the exemplars philosophers choose to illustrate the very concept of existence.

Defenders of states of affairs tell us that it is not enough simply to have the concrete electron e, and for e to be negatively charged. One must acknowledge the existence of a further object, the state of affairs *electron e's being negatively charged*. There is disagreement over how many states of affairs should be posited. Some posit a state of affairs *a's being F* whenever a is F. Some are more parsimonious and posit the state of affairs *a's being F* only when a is F, and a and F are fundamental. Some throw parsimony to the wind and posit the state of affairs *a's being F* even when it is false that a is F.

I have no knock-down argument against states of affairs. Indeed, there are so many different views on the nature of states of affairs that I doubt there is a single objection capable of ruling out all conceptions. My case against them is merely that they have been insufficiently motivated: for all that has been said, there is not strong enough reason for going beyond an ontology of concrete particulars. We do not need the unfamiliar entity *the fence's being brown*—the brown fence is enough. Nonetheless, while sceptical, I am cautiously sceptical. As I shall argue, there is a sense in which work still needs to be done by both parties to fully settle the issue.

2. States of Affairs and Common Sense

States of affairs are often motivated by pointing to the parts of ordinary thought and talk that involve quantification over or reference to states of affairs. For instance:

1. *Quine's being a Philosopher* obtains, while *Quine's being a Politician* does not[2].
2. There are two facts that the detective did not know.
3. There are two possible scenarios: either that Peter comes alone or that he brings Mary with him.
4. Martin might have had straight hair—that is a possible way he might have been.[3]
5. Every state has a well-defined energy.

In all these cases, something is referred to or quantified over—something that cannot be understood as an ordinary, concrete particular. Let us call these things—whatever they are—*states of affairs*. Does the fact that 1–5 are platitudes show that states of affairs are, after all, as much part of our common-sense ontology as concrete particulars? If so, then my initial scepticism about states of affairs is misconceived from the outset. After all, common sense should be the starting point of any serious ontological enquiry: if states of affairs are common-sense entities, then the onus is on the sceptic to argue that they lead to some kind of trouble.

But the linguistic evidence is weaker than it at first appears. First, the evidence does not point towards a single ontological category. A single technical term, 'states of affairs', has been introduced to cover a disparate set of metaphysical kinds. In 1, we are asked to believe in things that do and do not *obtain;* in 2, it is facts—entities corresponding to true sentences—which are mentioned: but no fact corresponds to the non-obtaining *Quine's being a politician*. In 3, we find talk of possible scenarios. These are different again: *the grass's being red and green all over* does not obtain—but this is no *possible* scenario. Sentence 4 talks of a *way* that someone could be. But a way that someone could be is a *property* of an object—something that an object may or may not instantiate as opposed to something that may or may not *obtain*. 'Object o instantiated state of affairs S' doesn't even sound grammatical. Admittedly, for theoretical reasons, we may decide to identify possible ways with states of affairs: but that will result in linguistic revision, a change of our linguistic practice—it will demand that we assent to things we did not, at the common-sense level, assent to. The platitudes do not all point to a common, ontological item.

Second, the linguistic evidence is equivocal. It is easy to get the folk to assent to 'the table exists', 'the barking dog exists', 'Quine exists': such existential statements about concrete particulars *are* platitudinous. But existential state-ments about states of affairs are not: 'The state of affairs of *Quine's being a politician* exists' scarcely sounds well formed, let alone a platitude. Yet it is supposed to be a straightforward implication of the platitude '*Quine's being a philosopher* does not obtain'. True, the folk are not logically omnipotent—the property of being platitudinous is not preserved across logical implication. Yet the implication is a one liner—if the first sentence were ontologically com-mitting, the conclusion should at least be *almost* as much of a platitude as the premise.

Finally, reading our common-sense commitments off the surface structure of ordinary language leads to trouble. For example, consider holes. There are perfectly good sentences of English which existentially quantify over holes: 'There is at least one hole in the bucket'. There are perfectly good sentences of English which numerically quantify over holes: 'There are exactly three holes in the bucket'. There are sentences which contain terms for holes and which predicate things of the hole: 'The biggest hole in this bucket are all circular'. There are sentences which contain relational predicates of holes: 'The holes in this bucket are all bigger than the holes in that bucket'. The language with which we talk of holes is entirely analogous to the language we use to talk about ordinary concrete particulars, such as tables and chairs.

Yet it is a confusion to conclude that it is part of common sense that there exist such things as holes. A hole is not an addition in our ontology—it is a *lack* of ontology. 'There is a hole in the bucket' correctly describes the bucket pre-cisely because it is *not* the case that there is something where there should be! Holes are absences, lacks, omissions—there is a hole in the bucket not because there exists a special kind of entity located in the bucket, but because an ordi-nary object is *lacking* from the bucket. Ontological seriousness about holes, whatever Bargle may say,[4] is the very antithesis of a common-sense position.

3. Grounding the Platitudes

While it might be acknowledged that the existence of states of affairs is not part of common sense, it may still be argued that the platitudes do exert a kind of pressure on the sceptic. After all, even the most austere nominalist should recognise that, under the right conditions, there is *something* right about sen-tences 1–5. Simply dismissing all such thought and talk as false simply because the sceptic rejects their existential commitments wouldn't do justice to what is right or platitudinous about them.

Agreed—outright rejection fails to explain the role and function of thought and talk about states of affairs. A better response would be to try and para-phrase away reference and quantification to states of affairs, the paraphrases capturing what is right or important in the original sentences. For example, '*Quine's being a philosopher* obtains' can be captured by the simple 'Quine is a philosopher' without loss. But the other sentences cannot be so easily paraphrased and the sceptic runs the risk of pursuing ever more baroque constructions.

I prefer a different approach: the metaphysician should accommodate what is platitudinous in such sentences by showing that they can be grounded in a world which contains no states of affairs.[5] In accommodating 1–5, concessions about the nature of reality must be made. A world where Quine is not a philosopher is not a world which can ground 'Quine's being a philosopher obtains'. By contrast, a world in which Quine exists and Quine is a philosopher *is* a world which grounds this sentence—moreover, it is a world which grounds the sentence without positing a distinct ontological category: *states of affairs*. All that is required is that Quine exist, and that he be a philosopher.

The requirement that the platitudes be merely grounded allows the sceptic to avoid some of the difficulties that beset the attempt to find paraphrases. Consider sentence 2a: 'There are two facts the detective did not know: that grass is green and that snow is white'. For this sentence, paraphrase is easy: 'The detective did not know that grass is green and did not know that snow is white'. But in 2 above, the detective's ignorance is not specified: for all that 2 says, it could equally well be grounded by a world where he did not know the shapes of Jupiter and Mars. Now, due to our contingent limitations, a complete description of the detective's knowledge may be beyond us: we may not know exactly what it is the detective does not know and—if he possesses concepts we lack—we may lack the linguistic resources to describe his knowledge. Nevertheless, we can still recognise that a full and complete description of the detective's epistemological situation would take the following form: 'The detective knows that P & he knows that Q . . . and does not know that R and does not know that S . . . '. Whether or not there were two facts the Detective did not know is fully determined by a world which satisfied this conjunction. Yet there is nothing in this conjunction which refers to or quantifies over facts: the only ontological commitment is to the detective himself. While we may not possess this ideal description, we know enough about its form to recognise that the reality which grounds 2 is committed to nothing more than the detective himself. The sceptic can recognise and understand how the sentence is grounded, and so acknowledge what is platitudinous in the sentence, without having to accept states of affairs.

Sentences 3 and 4 bring something new to the table: modality. This means that, in elucidating the ground of these sentences—that is, in outlining the ideal description that describes a world which grounds such sentences—the sceptic must take a stance on the nature of modality. This is a huge topic in and of itself whatever our attitude to states of affairs. Nonetheless, I take the following view to be at least coherent and plausible: that the modal modifiers are not disguised quantifiers over worlds, that the box and the diamond may be taken as *operators* rather than predicates, and that certain modal truths, such as 'it is possible that a is F', may express fundamental truths about the world, not to be analysed or explained in terms of anything more basic. On this view, an ideal and exhaustive description of modal reality consists of a sentence of the form '◊Gb & ◊Hcd. . . . ', and that some such sentence is an exhaustive description of modal reality.

With this in mind, consider 4: '*Martin's having straight hair* is a possible way Martin might have been'. This is grounded by a world in which it is indeed possible that Martin have had straight hair. As for 3, this is grounded by a world in which it is both possible that Peter comes alone and is possible that Peter brings Mary with him. Again, in no case are *states of affairs* required.

As before, the sceptic will not always actually be able to give a complete description of the reality that grounds a particular statement. Consider, for instance, the weaker statement 3a, 'there are two possible scenarios' and nothing more is said. This statement may be grounded by a world in which it is both possible that Peter comes alone, and possible that Peter brings Mary with him. But even when it is not possible for Peter to bring Mary with him, the original statement can still be true—perhaps because it is both possible that Peter come alone and possible that Peter bring Sally with him. The sceptic may not know which, if either, of the two descriptions is correct. Without the relevant information, we cannot say. But whichever of the two it may be, he can recognise that the statement is grounded in a modal reality which contains no such things as states of affairs. Even without paraphrase, the sceptic's conception of modal reality allows him to accommodate what is platitudinous in 3a.

We shall turn to 5 below when we have a better understanding of the role states play in science.

4. States of Affairs: Theoretical Utility

A different way to argue for states of affairs appeals to some theoretical role that they play in science or philosophy. The comparison here is with the Quine-Putnam Indispensability argument: mathematical entities are argued to exist because of the indispensable role they play in scientific theories—our theories are simpler, more systematic, have greater theoretical virtue when they are formulated in mathematical terms. Can an analogous case be constructed for states of affairs?

The theoretical roles allegedly fulfilled by states of affairs are many and varied. For Armstrong, states of affairs are needed to accommodate the intuition that every truth has a truthmaker (Armstrong 1997). Forbes suggests that states of affairs are needed to be the bearers of modalities (Forbes 1989). For Plantinga, states of affairs give us the best theory of possible worlds (Plantinga 1974). But in such cases, I find myself sceptical that the alleged work needs to be done, or that the entities posited do so in a way that really increases overall theoretical utility. Why should 'Quine is a philosopher' have a *truthmaker*? We have Quine, and that he is a philosopher—I see no reason to think that the truth requires anything more from reality. Nor do I see a reason for thinking that the modalities should be understood as analogous to ordinary categorical properties, requiring them to have some bearer. And Plantinga ultimately must posit haecceities as well as states of affairs, thus undermining the total theoretical simplicity of his overall theory.

Part of the power of the Quine-Putnam argument comes from the fact that it is not merely philosophical theory which requires mathematical objects, but *scientific* theory. In this section, I examine whether there is a case for states of affairs from the role they play in science.

Now, cases can be found where scientists, in explaining their theories in ordinary language, employ quantify over or refer to states of affairs. Yet the ontological commitments of ordinary language do not change just because a scientist is using it. Insofar as the reference and quantification over states of ordinary language can be understood as grounded in a reality which does not reify states of affairs, the issues of the previous section simply reappear. Of course, the scientist may tell us 'the cause of the explosion was the state of radioactive material: namely, the closeness of the two pieces of Uranium'. This is not a platitude of common sense, but an empirical discovery. Nevertheless, the sceptic can maintain that what has been discovered is that there was an explosion because the two pieces of Uranium were close: the scientist's statement is grounded by a world that does not involve such *things* as states. The scientist may tell us that he has discovered that H_2O naturally appears in three different states. If the sceptic believes that ice, water and steam are all appear naturally, and all are H_2O, he can accommodate the scientist's discovery.

When we turn from ordinary language to more formal scientific theory, the evidence that science requires the existence of states becomes weaker. Mathematics is ubiquitous in modern scientific theory: almost all serious scientific theories employ a large amount of mathematical machinery, and this machinery appears to be indispensable—a problem for the nominalist. By contrast, standard formulations of many scientific theories do not explicitly quantify or refer to states: Newton's theory of motion, Maxwell's theory of electromagnetism and Einstein's theory of relativity neither explicitly nor implicitly refer to such things as states. Material bodies, fields and—arguably—points of space-time may appear in the standard formulations of these theories—but not states of affairs.

Nonetheless, while talk of states of affairs may not be ubiquitous in genuine scientific theorising in the way that talk of numbers is, it is not entirely absent either. After all, serious scientific theories do employ and utilise the concept of a *state space*. The states in a state space correspond to ways a system could be so they are a natural candidate for philosopher's term 'state of affairs'—at least on one conception. So: does scientists' use of state space motivate the acceptance of states into our ontology?

As a first step in addressing this question, we focus on a concrete example of the formal presentation of a state space in classical physics. Suppose we have a classical system of n (concrete) particles. Classical Newtonian physics allows that these particles may have various positions and possess various momenta. At a given moment, a system of n particles may be freely distributed in a three-dimensional space and the particles may have any arbitrary distribution of momenta. Given that there are n-particles, we can form the 6n-tuple <x1, y1, z1, x2, y2, z2,.... xn, yn, zn, px1, py1, pz1, px2, py2, pz2 ... pxn, pyn, pzn>. The various numbers in the 6n-tuple correspond to the spatial components of the positions and momenta of the n particles. (From here on, rather than writing out all the components, I'll abbreviate this to $<X1, X2 \ldots Xn, P1, P2 \ldots Pn>$, where Xj is a triple of numbers representing the x, y and z coordinates of the jth particle, and Pk is also a triple quantity representing the components of the momentum of the kth particle.) The collection of *all* these 6n-tuples is the state space of the n-particle system[6].

As it stands, this formal presentation of state space is committed at most to mathematical entities. But the mathematics, of course, represents some kind of physical reality. Understanding the *ontology* to which scientific theories employing state space is committed requires the following: (a) an account of what the state space represents—a physical *interpretation*; (b) a demonstration that this interpretation can do justice to the role state space plays in scientific theory.

One way to interpret state space would be to regard each element as denoting a distinct physical entity—the *state* of a system. This yields an ontologically unparsimonious conception of states: the state space contains non-denumerably many elements and the vast majority of these states are not realised by any actual system. A less extravagant interpretation would be the following: a given n-tuple $<X1, X2 \ldots Xn, P1, P2 \ldots Pn>$ represents a system of n particles, with the first particle in position $X1$ and with momentum $P1$, the second particle in position $X2$ and with momentum $P2 \ldots$ and so on. This involves no reification of states. Other meaningful physical quantities, such as the energy of a system, are represented by mathematical functions of the positions and momenta. This interpretation is perfectly adequate for dealing with parts of science where elements of the state space are used to represent actual systems.

But the content of a scientific theory goes beyond propositions involving particular systems represented by elements of state space: important information is conveyed by propositions involving the *entire* state space—independently of whether or not the elements correspond to any actual system. For instance, the following may be important truths about a theory:

5. Every state possesses a well-defined energy.
6. There is at least one state in which the total momentum of the system has a value P. The physical significance of these claims cannot be understood

simply in terms of the properties of actual systems. As a matter of contingent fact, there may be no system of n particles whose momentum has value p. But the existence of such states in state space may still be an important fact about the relevant physical theory. It seems that a further interpretative move must be made if we are to account for the significance of such claims without reifying states.

I say that claims 5 and 6 are best understood as saying something about what kinds of systems *could* and *must* exist, compatible with the relevant physical theory. Claim 5 should be understood as a statement about what is physically necessary according to the theory, 6 a statement about what is physically possible. It's not just the case that the various elements of state space represent systems which such and such properties: the space itself represent all and only the possible systems that are compatible with the relevant theory. But this is not to say that the elements of state space literally represent various possible states, each element corresponding to a different entity. Rather, the modal content of the theory is better understood as completely described by giant conjunction of sentences of the form 'it is physically possible that n particles occupy positions $X1 \ldots Xn$ and possess momenta $P1 \ldots P2$', one conjunct for each element of the state space. It is the conjunction of these truths—plus the fact that it is physically necessary that n particles instantiate one of these conjunctions—that expresses the modal content of the state space.

My claim is that this large conjunction is a complete and exhaustive description of what is physically possible, according to the theory. The physicist's statements about the properties and relationships about states—at least as they appear for classical physics—can (I claim) all be understood as grounded by a modal reality which is fully and exhaustively described by a statement which does not reify states.

To defend this claim, let us examine what, at first sight, seems to be a problematic case. Consider the sentence

7. State S is a State of Least Possible Energy

This statement seems to *relate* different states, comparing them with regards to the energy they carry. The quantification over states in 5 and 6 could be easily paraphrased away in terms of modal operators. But how can the obtaining of relations such as *less energy* be understood if, as the sceptic maintains, there are no genuine relata? How can the sceptic make room for what is physically right in 7?

(The need to accommodate statements such as 7 is physically important: statements involving comparisons between different states can play a significant role in physics. For instance, the fact that a certain state is minimal with respect to a certain quantity plays a central role in Lagrangian versions of classical mechanics. In such presentations, the dynamical laws are derived by comparing histories of varying sequences of states. A quantity called the *action* is defined and various sequences of states can be said to expend a certain amount of action. For any state A and any state B, the evolution which actually occurs is given by that path through state space which *minimises* the action that is expended in the evolution.[7] While it is possible to take such a formulation as nothing more than an elegant or attractive way to derive the standard laws of motion, it can be argued that the Lagrangian formulation is *explanatory* in a way in which the standard formulations are not: it is precisely *because* [so the thought goes] the actual history of history of states *minimises* the action that the dynamical laws have their particular form. It is precisely by recognising that the actual action spent is less than that spent by any other possible path through state space that we see what is special and distinctive of the actual laws, why it is they have the form they do. See Lyon and Colyvan [2008] for further discussion.)

Fortunately for the sceptic, the relation *less energy* is an internal relation: whether or not the relation holds supervenes upon the properties of the two systems. Because of this, 7 can be grounded.

Let us illustrate by considering a (unrealistically) small state space. Suppose a theory's state space for n particles contained just two elements: S1 and S2. Let us also use 'S1' and 'S2' as abbreviations for the corresponding descriptions of the positions and momenta of an n particle system. Then the conjunction describing modal reality according to this theory is very simple: it's possible that there be n particles with positions and momenta S1; and it's possible that there be n particles with position and momenta S2. Now, the distribution of momenta determines the energy of a system: necessarily, a system of n particles with positions and momenta S1 has energy E1; necessarily, a system of n particles with positions and momenta S2 has energy E2. As *less energy* is an internal relation, fixing the values of E1 and E2 alone fixes which of the two has less energy.

Now, for concreteness, let us suppose that E1 is less than E2. Since there are only two conjuncts in our description, and our description is an exhaustive description of modal reality, according to the theory, it follows that it is physically necessary that any n particle system either satisfies S1 or S2. If it is physically necessary that a system satisfy S1 or S2 then, as E1 is less than E2, a system which satisfies S1 must have the least possible energy. Claim 7 is grounded. Of course, state space usually contains more elements than two. But that only affects the size of the conjunction—that a particular state is correctly described as the one that carries the least possible energy can be grounded in exactly the same way.

That we were able to ground statements comparing different states rested upon the relevant relations being internal. Is there reason for the sceptic to be optimistic that this is the always the case? Perhaps not. Up to now, we've considered state spaces for classical mechanics. State space for quantum mechanics, however, poses a new set of problems. In quantum mechanics, state space is a special kind of vector space called a Hilbert Space. As a vector space, various elements of the (mathematical) state spaces stand in various relations to each other: one particular state **a** may be the equal to $x\mathbf{b} + y\mathbf{c}$, (where x and y are complex numbers.) The fact that states can be linear combinations of other states is connected to one of the more puzzling aspects of quantum mechanics: understanding the sense in which a cat can be said to be simultaneously both alive and dead in various degrees. The fact that one vector is the mathematical sum of various other vectors is physically significant. But, worryingly for the sceptic, it is not at all clear how to ground the physical significance of these relations in terms of the kind of conjunctions of modal sentences we have so far examined.

So states earn their keep after all? This is too quick: the physical interpretation of quantum mechanics is *generally* unclear and contentious. It is not even clear how to interpret individual elements of the state space, let alone the relations that hold between them.[8] At a pragmatic level, elements of state space encode various probabilities, the expectation values of various quantities and the likely results of various possible measurements—but whether this is anything like a complete description of a way a system could be is a matter of contention. Whether they should even be realistically interpreted, or instead merely taken to correspond to the properties of an *ensemble* of systems, or a set of probability distributions, is a fiercely debated matter.

Still—*if* the states were to be realistically interpreted, and *if* the mathematical summation relation holding between the various vectors were best understood as representing a genuine, external relation, then a case for states emerges. If, for instance, the mathematical summation relation is best understood as corresponding to a literal composition relation, if the best way to understand a cat in a superposition being alive and being dead is as a state which is literally composed of two states—*the cat's being alive* and *the cat's being dead*—then our strategy for grounding scientific talk of states is in trouble. Of course, the composition here is not mereological composition: the summation relations do not obey the axioms of mereology.[9] But defenders of states of affairs have already accept non-mereological modes of composition for states of affairs (see Lewis 1986).

Still: the interpretational issues of quantum mechanics are severe and the physical interpretation of the mathematics of Hilbert space is unsettled. And I know of no interpretation which claims that summation does correspond to mereology. Much work still needs to be done by the defender of states to show that science must really posit this new ontological category. But what I hope this discussion shows is that there is still a lot of work to be done by *both* sides. While it is too quick to move from the observation that physical theory sometimes makes use of mathematical state space to the conclusion that physical theory is best or most naturally understood in terms of an ontology of states, we have given no argument here showing that *all* uses of states in *all* areas of science can be grounded in ways that would satisfy the nominalist. To fully settle the issue, a careful examination of detailed scientific theory, and the role and application of the concept of state within scientific theory, are needed. But in the absence of plausible examples from physics which require us to take the notion of a state with ontological seriousness, I remain (cautiously) sceptical of the existence of states of affairs.

Notes

1. Strawson (1950).
2. Plantinga (1974).
3. 3–4 are from Textor encyclopaedia article on states of affairs (2012).
4. See Lewis and Lewis 1970.
5. I sympathise to Armstrong's idea that, in ontology, we should look to see what makes our sentences true rather than the variables and referring terms in the sentences themselves (Armstrong 1997). But I resist Armstrong's reification of states of affairs. See Melia 2005 for more details.
6. Strictly speaking, this is called a phase space, which is a particular kind of state space in physics.
7. See Butterfield (2004).
8. Even physics textbooks urge caution about the interpretative issues: 'The concept of *state* is one of the most subtle and controversial concepts in quantum mechanics' (Ballentine 1998: 47).
9. For example, state **a** can be a sum of states **b**, **c** and **d**; while state **b** can be a sum of states that includes **a**.

References

Armstrong, D.M. 1997. *A World of States of Affairs*. Cambridge: Cambridge University Press.
Ballentine, Leslie E. 1998. *Quantum Mechanics: A Modern Development*. World Scientific: London.
Beebee, H. and J. Dodd. 2005. *Truthmakers, the Contemporary Debate*. Oxford: Oxford University Press.
Butterfield, J. 2004. "Some Aspects of Modality in Analytical Mechanics". In M. Stoltzner and P. Weingartner (eds.), *Formal Teleology and Causality*. Paderborn: Mentis. Available at Los Alamos arXive: http://arxiv.org/abs/physics/0210081.
Forbes, G. 1989. *Languages of Possibility*. Oxford: Basil Blackwell.
Lewis, D. 1986. "A Comment on Armstrong and Forrest." *Australasian Journal of Philosophy* 64: 92–93.
Lewis, D. and S. Lewis. 1970. "Holes." *Australasian Journal of Philosophy* 48: 206–212.
Lyon, A and M. Colyvan. 2008. "The Explanatory Power of Phase Spaces." *Philosophia Mathematica* 16: 227–243.
Melia, J. 2005. "Truth-Making without Truth-Makers". In H. Beebee and J. Dodd, 67–84.
Plantinga, A. 1974. *The Nature of Necessity*. Oxford: Clarendon Press.
Strawson, P. 1950. "Truth." *Proceedings of the Aristotelian Society* XXIV, 111–172.
Textor, Mark. 2012. "States of Affairs". In Edward N. Zalta (ed.), *The Stanford Encyclopedia of Philosophy*, Summer 2012 edition, http://plato.stanford.edu/archives/sum2012/entries/states-of-affairs/.

PART IV

Are There Any Indeterminate States of Affairs?

CHAPTER 7

Are There Indeterminate States of Affairs? Yes

JESSICA WILSON*

Many phenomena appear to be indeterminate. For example, we experience certain objects (clouds, mountains) as having imprecise boundaries; the future, it seems, might be genuinely open; on the orthodox interpretation of quantum mechanics, some properties of a system (e.g., position and momentum) cannot jointly have precise values. Here I'll compare two accounts on which some seeming indeterminacy, in these or other cases, is genuinely *metaphysical* indeterminacy (MI).

An important difference between the two accounts concerns whether MI is taken to require that states of affairs (SOAs) be indeterminate, where an SOA is a worldly state consisting, in the simplest case, of an object's having a property—say, the cat's being on the mat. On the approach favored by Barnes and Cameron in the companion piece to this article, every SOA is itself precise/determinate, and MI is a matter of its being *indeterminate* which *determinate* SOA obtains.[1] As Barnes (2010), puts it: "It's perfectly determinate that everything is precise, but [. . .] it's indeterminate which precise way things are" (622). Here, for example, what it is for a cloud to have an indeterminate boundary is for it to be indeterminate which precise boundary the cloud has. On the approach I favour, MI is a matter of its being *determinate*—or just plain true—that an *indeterminate* SOA obtains, where an indeterminate SOA is one whose constitutive object has a determinable property, but no unique determinate of that determinable. (I'll say more about determinables and determinates shortly.) Here, for example, what it is for a cloud to have an indeterminate boundary is for the cloud to have a determinable boundary property, but no unique determinate boundary property. Reflecting the structural difference in where MI is located, I call the first approach a 'meta-level' approach, and the second an 'object-level' approach.

In this chapter I have three aims. First is to note a further important difference between my and Barnes and Cameron's accounts, concerning whether MI is taken to induce propositional indeterminacy (§1). Second is to highlight and defend certain advantages of my account (§2). Third is to address certain of Barnes and Cameron's objections to my account (§3).

1. Preliminaries

I want to start by saying a bit more about my account. This will set up for the comparative assessment to follow, and also allow for some preliminary brush-clearing. The need for brush-clearing reflects Barnes and Cameron's supposition that MI is always reflected in a *proposition's* being indeterminate, and their further characterization of our views as differing over whether such propositional indeterminacy introduces, in addition to the usual 'demands' that propositions place on the world if they are to be true or false, a new kind of demand whose satisfaction is required if the proposition is to be indeterminate. On their preferred 'Unsettledness View', propositional indeterminacy due to MI does not introduce any new demands beyond those associated with truth or falsity—it is just indeterminate which of the usual demands is met. On what they call the 'Third-Way View', "propositions also make specific demands on the world for their indeterminacy", such that "[t]he world [. . .] settles what propositions are true, what ones are false, and what ones are indeterminate", and where what is required for a proposition to be indeterminate is "the obtaining of a special new kind of state of affairs: perhaps the state of an object indeterminately instantiating a familiar property, or perhaps the state of an object instantiating the non-familiar property of *being indeterminately F*" (123). They then offer certain concerns about a Third-Way view so construed, with my account being characterized as "a particularly interesting version" of such a view (127).

As will become clear, however, my account is not any kind of Third-Way view, for my account does not give rise to any indeterminate propositions, and so it is no part of my account that "propositions also make specific demands on the world for their indeterminacy" (123); nor does my account involve the positing of any "special new" SOAs of the sort just described. That my account is not a version of a Third-Way view will be relevant to the comparative assessment to come.

1.1. A Determinable-Based Object-Level Account

On my object-level account, MI is a matter of its being *determinate*—or just plain true—that an *indeterminate* SOA obtains, where what it is for an SOA to be MI is spelled out as follows:

> *Determinable-based MI*: What it is for a state of affairs *S* to be metaphysically indeterminate at a time *t* is for *S* to constitutively involve an object (more generally, entity) *O* such that (i) *O* has a determinable property *P* at *t*, and (ii) *O* does not have a unique determinate of *P* at *t*.[2]

Why look to determinables for insight into MI? To start, determinables are distinctively *unspecific* properties which admit of specification by determinate properties—e.g., the determinable *being coloured* may be determined by the determinate *being scarlet*; the determinable *being shaped* may be determined by the determinate *being rectangular*. Moreover, unlike other kinds of unspecific properties (e.g., disjunctions, genus properties), determinables are *irreducibly* imprecise—in particular, they are not reducible to any complex combinations of precise determinates (see Wilson 2012). Hence, determinables are potentially suited to provide a basis for understanding MI.

Now, it has been traditionally supposed that when an object possesses a determinable property at a time, it also possesses a unique—one and only one—determinate at that time, at a given level of specification. However, as I discuss in Wilson 2013, the traditional assumption is too strong, and should be rejected as generally characterizing determinables and determinates.

Consider colour, the paradigmatic determinable property. Is it really the case that if an object is coloured, it must have one and only one determinate of colour (at a given level of specification)? The colour of an iridescent feather, which shifts from red to blue depending on the angle of viewing, suggests otherwise. As Johnsgard (1997) says:

> The highly iridescent feathers of the hummingbird gorgets are among the most specialized of all bird feathers. [...] The colors do not directly depend on selective pigment absorption and reflection [...] Rather, they depend on interference coloration, such as that resulting from the colors seen in an oil film or soap-bubble. [...] Thus, a gorget may appear ruby red when seen with a beam of light coming from directly behind the eye, but as the angle is changed the gorget color will shift from red to blue and finally to black, as the angle of incidence increases.

Such a case suggests that determination may be relative to perspective or other circumstances. Moreover, it suggests that determination may be a *multiply relativized phenomenon*: multiple such circumstances may be in place at a time, as when, for example, you and I both look at an iridescent feather and you see red, while I see blue. In such a case of multiple relativized determination, the feather is coloured at a time *t*—it has the determinable property *being coloured* at *t*. But it would be arbitrary, hence inappropriate, to pick one of the determinate properties of this determinable—either *being red* or *being blue*—as being 'the' determinate shade had by the feather at *t*; and this would be inappropriate whether or not the candidate determinates are relativized. So the case of an iridescent feather is one where it is reasonable to assume that an object has a determinable property (namely, *colour*), but no *unique* determinate of that property. Note also that if only one of us were looking at the feather, it wouldn't thereby become less arbitrary or more appropriate to attribute a single colour determinate to the feather. As such, cases of actual or possible multiple relativized determination show that the traditional supposition that when an object possesses a determinable property at a time, it must possess a unique determinate at that time, is not generally correct.

The iridescent feather case shows that the conditions of *Determinable-based MI* may be satisfied due to there being *too many* candidate determinates of the determinable. This route to satisfaction of the conditions corresponds to what I call 'glutty' MI, and in my 2013 paper I suggest that this kind of implementation of a determinable-based account makes good sense of indeterminate macro-object boundaries. Take Mount Everest.[3] Intuitively, Mount Everest does not have a precise boundary; as Tye (1990) says, "common sense has it that the world contains countries, mountains, deserts, and islands [. . .] and these items certainly do not appear to be perfectly precise" (215). And science tells us that the same is true for macro-objects that appear to be more distinctly spatially individuated, such as tables and statues. On my account, such cases are treated as follows:

> *Determinable-based MI (macro-object boundaries)*: What it is for a macro-object *O* to have an indeterminate boundary is for it to be determinately the case (or just plain true) that (i) *O* has a determinable boundary property *P* but (ii) *O* does not have a unique determinate of *P* at *t*.

Why think that mountains, clouds, tables, and statues can have a determinable boundary property, but no unique determinate boundary property? In my 2013 paper, I tell a longer story, but the short story here is that these sorts of macro-objects and their properties are intimately dependent upon—realized by—multiple lower-level aggregates and their properties. In the case of Mount Everest, for example, there are multiple distinct but overlapping aggregates of rock, each of which has a comparatively precise boundary property which is plausibly seen as a determinate of Mount Everest's determinable boundary property.[4] The structure of the case here is similar to that of the iridescent feather: it is reasonable to assume that Mount Everest has a single determinable boundary property, which is determined, at any given time, by multiple more specific boundary properties. Here too, it would be arbitrary to single out any one of these determinate boundary properties as that which is *uniquely* had by Mount Everest.[5] Hence, cases of macro-object boundary MI can be seen as conforming, in glutty fashion, to the conditions of *Determinable-based MI*.

The failure of the traditional supposition of unique determination also makes room for 'gappy' satisfaction of the conditions in *Determinable-based MI*—namely, if *too few* or *no* determinates of the determinable are instantiated, even as a relativized matter, by either the object in the indeterminate SOA or any other object(s). A gappy implementation handles other cases of MI. For example, in my 2013 paper, I argue that the open future can be treated in gappy determinable-based terms (an application to which I will return down the line), and Bokulich (2014) and Wolff (2015) each suggest that a gappy determinable-based implementation represents a promising approach to cases of quantum MI.[6]

Summing up: on a determinable-based object-level account, MI involves the obtaining of an indeterminate SOA, where an indeterminate SOA is an SOA whose constituent object (more generally, entity) has a determinable property, but no unique determinate of that determinable. There are two ways in which the pattern of instantiation of properties at issue here may occur: first, if there are too many candidate determinates of the determinable at issue, à la glutty MI; second, if there are too few (or no) candidate determinates, à la gappy MI.

1.2. Is My Determinable-Based Account a 'Third-Way View'? No

As previously mentioned, Barnes and Cameron characterize my determinable-based account as a version of a 'Third-Way view', and so take their concerns with a Third-Way view to also apply to my account. We are now in position to see, however, that my account is not a Third-Way view.

Again, on their schematic characterization, MI of whatever variety is registered in a *proposition's* being indeterminate. This reflects their characterizing MI in terms of propositional indeterminacy that remains even after semantic and epistemic indeterminacy is removed:

> [W]hat of cases where it is indeterminate whether a proposition is true or false? [. . .] By worldly indeterminacy we mean indeterminacy that remains even once we've specified exactly what proposition it is we're

asking about, and which is a matter of how reality itself is, not simply a matter of how we know it to be.

(121)

They then characterize the difference between an Unsettledness view and a Third-Way view, which difference is supposed to track a difference between our views, as reflecting a difference in how this remaining indeterminacy in propositions is treated: a Third-Way view takes this remaining propositional indeterminacy to introduce, in addition to the usual 'demands' that propositions place on the world if the proposition is to be true or false, a new kind of 'demand' whose satisfaction is required if the proposition is to be indeterminate, whereas an Unsettledness view takes this remaining propositional indeterminacy to reflect just that it's primitively unsettled which of the usual demands is met.

Now, the first problem here is that I do not take cases of MI to be associated with indeterminate propositions (or any other kind of representational entity). On my account, it is SOAs, not propositions, that are indeterminate; and—importantly—the sense in which SOAs are indeterminate does not render any propositions indeterminate. Consider, for example, my treatment of Mount Everest's indeterminate boundary. Here it is true that Mount Everest has the determinable boundary property, and for any unrelativized determinate boundary property, it is false that Mount Everest has that property. As such, it is false, not indeterminate, that Mount Everest has a precise boundary. Relatedly, it is not indeterminate that (or whether) Mount Everest has precise boundary #326—again, for any (unrelativized) precise boundary, it is false, not indeterminate, that (or whether) Mount Everest has that precise boundary. As for the relativized determinates: if it makes sense to take Mount Everest to have relativized precise boundaries (which it might not; see note 5), then these relativized attributions will be either true or false, depending on whether they conform to the facts; if this doesn't make sense, such attributions will all be false.[7] Similarly for cases where the conditions in *Determinable-based MI* arise due to the gappy absence of determinates of a given determinable—any associated propositions will be either true or false.[8]

Since my account does not give rise to any indeterminate propositions, it does not introduce any third kind of demand whose satisfaction is required for propositions to be indeterminate. Relatedly, it does not posit a third 'indeterminate' category of truth value, or an indeterminacy operator on propositions, or any other piece of semantic machinery that would suggest that propositions are ever anything other than true or false. There is nothing new, semantically speaking, in a determinable-based account of MI.

One might be concerned (as David Balcarras was) that maintaining the falsity of both 'the cat is alive' and 'the cat is dead' would involve rejecting an instance of the law of excluded middle (LEM)—namely, 'the cat is alive or the cat is not alive'. But in fact LEM is not violated here. The concern presupposes that if 'the cat is dead' is false, it follows that 'the cat is not alive' is also false, by substitution of 'dead' with the supposedly equivalent expression 'not alive'. But under conditions of gappy MI, 'dead' and 'not alive' are not equivalent, for under these conditions not being alive is compatible with not being dead, either; so the substitution is not licensed. Moreover, since from the falsity of 'the cat is alive' the truth of 'the cat is not alive' *does* follow, irrespective of whether conditions of gappy MI are in place, the instance of LEM at issue— 'the cat is alive or the cat is not alive'—is guaranteed to be true in virtue of the truth of the second disjunct. So a determinable-based treatment of gappy MI poses no threat to LEM. Thanks to Patrick Todd for discussion here; his paper (forthcoming) served as some inspiration for this approach, though our strategies are not completely isomorphic.

Though my account does not impose any new demands on propositions, might it be a Third-Way view at least in being, as Barnes and Cameron take Third-Way views to be, committed to "the obtaining of a special new kind of state of affairs: perhaps the state of an object *indeterminately instantiating* a familiar property, or perhaps the state of an object instantiating the *non-familiar* property of *being indeterminately F*" (123)? No. As above, my account is indeed committed to indeterminate SOAs, but these do not involve unfamiliar notions such as indeterminate instantiation or properties such as *being indeterminately F*; on the contrary, I explicitly disavow such notions (2013: 364). Rather, as I say in my 2013 paper, "On a determinable-based account, MI ultimately comes down to a certain pattern of possession of a determinable property" (382). We are already committed to determinables and determinates, and to objects (e.g., iridescent feathers) instantiating the sort of pattern that is, on my account, constitutive of MI. On my account, indeterminate SOAs are not "a special new kind of state of affairs"—they are just a subset of the usual SOAs, involving ordinary properties and ordinary instantiation, to which we are already committed. There is nothing new, metaphysically speaking, in a determinable-based account of MI.

So my account is not a Third-Way view; but neither is it an Unsettledness view; hence Barnes and Cameron's characterization of the options for treating MI leaves out my account. An upshot is that one of the three concerns that they raise against a Third-Way view clearly does not apply to my account—namely, the concern that "[t]he defender of the Third-Way View [. . .] must reject bivalence, or she must reject the plausible link between truth-value and the world meeting the demands for that truth-value" (125). As above, my account is straightforwardly compatible with bivalence—with every (meaningful) proposition's being true or false. Beyond this, Barnes and Cameron's discussion still usefully engages with my account, for as we'll see in the next two sections, the concerns that they raise specifically for my account do not hinge on its being a Third-Way view, and their second and third concerns with a Third-Way view can be massaged into concerns for my account.

2. Advantages of a Determinable-Based Object-Level Account

I next turn to observing three advantages of my account of MI over Barnes and Cameron's account: intelligibility, reducibility, and systematicity.

Barnes and Cameron nicely characterize two of these advantages. They first observe that my account has a "conceptual" advantage, in appealing to pretheoretically and independently understood notions, in such a way as to render MI intelligible:

> [T]here are two big advantages to Wilson's Third-Way View over our own Unsettledness View, one conceptual and one metaphysical, and both a result of the fact that our own view is thoroughly non-reductive concerning indeterminacy. The conceptual advantage is this: nobody who understands the machinery of determinates and determinable can fail to understand Wilson when she says that the world is metaphysically indeterminate. She has told you exactly what that means: it is for a certain kind of property to be instantiated without a certain [I would add, unique] other kind of property to be instantiated. If you understand what she means by such properties—if you grasp the determinate/ determinable distinction—then there is simply no room for not understanding worldly indeterminacy. Our own account, by contrast, makes ineliminable appeal to the notion of indeterminacy when we tell you how the world is. When p is indeterminate, we tell you that either the demands for p's truth or the demands for p's falsity are met, it is simply indeterminate which. Someone who is sceptical about the very idea of worldly indeterminacy is of course not going to be helped by this.
>
> (127–128)

They next observe that my account has a "metaphysical" advantage, in offering an ontologically reductive account of MI:

> The metaphysical advantage to Wilson's view is related. Just as we see indeterminacy as conceptually basic, so do we see the phenomenon as part of the fundamental bedrock of reality. [. . .] Wilson, by contrast, offers an ontological reduction of indeterminacy: *what it is* to be indeterminate is for a certain determinable to be had without a unique associated determinate being had. In giving us a *what it is* claim, she thereby avoids the need to think of reality as having primitive structure corresponding to indeterminacy. This is an advantage over our view. . . .
>
> (128, emphasis in the original)

I also observe a third advantage—namely, that a determinable-based account is desirably systematic. A meta-level account, in taking MI to be unsettledness between determinate options, presupposes that there *are* determinate options, and so cannot accommodate cases of gappy MI, where more determinate options are simply not available. Hence it is that (as argued in Darby [2010], Skow [2010], and Calosi and Wilson [in progress]) a meta-level account cannot accommodate orthodox quantum MI. By way of contrast, *Determinable-based MI* can be satisfied in either glutty or gappy fashion, and so has resources enabling it to accommodate both varieties of MI.

Barnes and Cameron go on, however, to raise a concern that, were it to stick, would undermine all three advantages. To secure the benefits of intelligibility and reducibility, they note, my account needs to accommodate all plausible cases of MI; otherwise, it would not count as characterizing *what it is* for there to be MI. They then mention three cases of seeming MI which they find implausible to treat in determinable-based terms, because, they claim, the needed determinable is either unavailable or too unusual to count as appealing to our familiar understanding of determinable and determinate properties. Were I to preserve the 'what it is' claim by denying that these are genuine cases of MI, this would, they suggest, be "a cost that is not worth paying" (129); I moreover add that any unprincipled such denials would undermine the supposed systematicity of a determinable-based account.

Their first case involves the indeterminate existence of an object or entity *A*:

This certainly does not look like a case that fits into the determinate/ determinable model, for there is no determinable that has existence and non-existence as determinates. And even if there were, it would surely be wrong to say that the indeterminacy of A's existence consists in its having this determinable—*having some state of being*, say—without having either of those determinates. For in saying that *A* has the determinable, we are *presupposing* the existence of *A*, and it's not even settled that there *is* such a thing.

(129, emphasis in the original)

Here I maintain that there is a determinable having existence and non-existence as determinates, and that this determinable is had, not by the entity *A* whose existence is MI, but by some other entity—e.g., the world, a field, a region of world or field, an aggregate of atoms, or the like. Note that there is nothing especially unusual in there being determinables having existence and non-existence as determinates; indeed, such determinables are arguably posited as properties of quantum vacuums, which "contain fluctuations, transitions between something and nothing in which potential existence can be transformed into real existence by the addition of energy" (Browne 1990).

If scientists can posit determinables involving "potential existence", so can metaphysicians.[9]

A second case involves the open future:

> Are we meant to hold that there is a determinable *having a future* that the world has, without having any determinate of the form *having such-and-such a particular future*? To say this just doesn't seem to be using our familiar notion of determinates and determinables.
>
> (129–130, emphasis in the original)

Here again I maintain that there's no special difficulty with positing the needed determinables. In my 2013 paper, I discuss a determinable-based implementation of the open future in detail; roughly, on my treatment, for the future to be open *vis-à-vis* the obtaining of a given event (say, a sea battle) is for it to presently be true that a determinable property will be instantiated (say, the outcome of a negotiation) and, for each determinate of that determinable (a decision to conduct a sea battle, a decision not to conduct a sea battle), for it to presently be false that that determinate will be instantiated. Here the determinable (*being the outcome of a negotiation*) is of a familiar variety. If there is something unusual about my treatment, it reflects that I implement a gappy approach to open future MI, such that it turns out that future contingents are all false; here I follow Todd (forthcoming) in thinking that this is actually quite intuitive, once one registers that there isn't presently anything to make either claim true.[10]

The last case is that of indeterminate identity of two objects or entities *A* and *B*. Here Barnes and Cameron say:

> [I]dentity and distinctness don't look like determinates of some more general determinable in the way that scarlet and crimson are determinates of red.
>
> (129)

Here I am inclined to deny that there is metaphysically indeterminate identity, for independent reasons. Many philosophers find indeterminate identity problematic—indeed, given certain suppositions, incoherent (following Evans 1983). Moreover, as I discuss in my 2013 paper, seeming commitment to indeterminate identity arises against the backdrop of a meta-level account, which I reject.[11] So even granting that a determinable-based account doesn't naturally treat indeterminate identity, this restriction doesn't undermine the aforementioned advantages of intelligibility, reducibility, and systematicity that my account enjoys.

3. Objections to a Determinable-Based Account of MI

I now want to consider and respond to two potential objections to my account, with a comparative assessment of Barnes and Cameron's approach in mind.

3.1. The Objection from Changing the Intuitive Subject

Barnes and Cameron object that Third-Way views fail to accommodate "the intuitive thought that indeterminacy is a matter of unsettledness between two options, rather than the introduction of a third option" (123):

> The phenomenon of indeterminacy is unsettledness as to which of the two exhaustive options obtains. The Unsettledness View secures this thought. When *p* is indeterminate, either the demands for the truth of *p* are met, or the demands for the falsity of *p* are met. It is simply unsettled which. The Third-Way View, by contrast, responds to the phenomenon of indeterminacy by introducing a third option [. . .] that is not amongst the states we would accept prior to our theorizing about indeterminacy [. . .] [H]ow does it help to just introduce a third option?
>
> (124)

As stated, this concern doesn't directly apply to my account, since as previously, my account does not posit a state "that is not amongst the states we would accept prior to our theorizing about indeterminacy". It is true, however, that my account does not characterize MI in meta-level terms, as involving unsettledness about *which* determinate option obtains; so the broader concern about missing the intuitive mark, or changing the intuitive subject, does apply to my account.

My response is three-fold. First, I deny that it is generally intuitive to characterize MI in meta-level terms. Recall Tye's (1996) observation: "It is also part and parcel of our commonsense view that [mountains, deserts, and clouds] are not perfectly precise, that they have fuzzy boundaries" (215). A common-sense—that is, intuitive—conception according to which mountains and other macro-objects "are not perfectly precise" and "have fuzzy boundaries" seems to me naturally read as characterizing such objects as *determinately failing* to have precise boundaries, not as being such that it is indeterminate *which* precise boundary they have. Nor do other cases of MI intuitively involve, as Barnes and Cameron claim, "unsettledness about which of the two exhaustive options obtains" (124). For example, if the future options are genuinely open, then intuitively, *none* of them "obtain"— the future hasn't happened yet, after all. Or so it seems to me.

Second, an intuitive conception of MI as involving unsettledness about which determinate option obtains gets it clearly wrong (as above) about quantum MI, which for theoretical reasons cannot be understood in meta-level terms. More generally, intuitions are data rather than decisive. As per usual, we need to consider what account of MI does best at satisfying various theoretical desiderata, including being able to handle the full range of cases; and here a determinable-based account has the advantage over a meta-level account in that the former, but not the latter, has resources to handle gappy as well as glutty cases of MI.

Third, even if some cases of seeming MI are intuitively characterized as involving something like 'unsettledness between determinate options', a glutty application of a determinable-based account can accommodate the force of such intuitions and the associated 'unsettledness' conception of MI. Consider again the treatment of boundary MI on which Mount Everest has a determinable boundary property, but—thanks to the presence of multiple realizing aggregates of rock—no unique determinate of that determinable. Here the existence of multiple determinates accommodates the intuitive idea that "[e]ach option has some pull"; that the unrelativized determinates are mutually exclusive accommodates the intuitive idea that "[the options] can't both obtain, as the states are exclusive"; and that it doesn't make sense to pick out one of these determinates as the unique one had by Mount Everest accommodates the intuitive idea that "there are [multiple] options but reality is not so simple as to have settled on one" (124). More generally, the phenomenon of multiple relativized determination provides a metaphysical basis for making sense of intuitions that (some cases of) MI involve reality's being unsettled between determinate options—not because reality is primitively unsettled about *which* of the determinate options obtains, but rather because these determinate options can be had, at best, in *relativized* fashion. So far as accommodating intuition, then, I think our accounts are fairly on a par.

3.2. The Objection from Ontological Commitment

Barnes and Cameron say:

> A third benefit accruing to the Unsettledness View is that it is entirely non-committal with respect to one's broader metaphysics. You can accept any account you like as to what states potentially make up the world. The Unsettledness View will not force you to alter that account; it will simply ask you to accept that it can be unsettled which states obtain. You can take whatever metaphysical story you like—the world consists of Armstrongian states of affairs; of atoms in the void; of ideas in the mind of God; etc.—the Unsettledness View will be compatible with that

metaphysics: it simply says that it is indeterminate *which* states involving those things obtain. The Third-Way View, by contrast, demands a metaphysics that allows for the special states of affairs associated with indeterminacy.

(125–126)

Here again, the concern as stated does not apply to my account, which does not involve introducing any "special" SOAs of the sort (again, involving indeterminate instantiation, or properties such as *being indeterminately F*) that Barnes and Cameron associate with Third-Way views. Nor does the fact that a determinable-based account invokes reference to objects, properties (including determinables and determinates), and associated SOAs (involving objects having properties) in itself show that my account is more "ontologically committal" than theirs. As Barnes and Cameron note about their own talk of SOAs:

> What we go on to say using 'states of affairs' talk should be acceptable, suitably translated, to those who favor a more austere ontology than Armstrong's.

(120)

The same can be said of the notions at issue in a determinable-based account.

If there is a distinctive ontological cost of my account, it is that it requires acceptance of determinables as irreducible to determinates. But I don't see that Barnes and Cameron's account has a comparative advantage here, for their account also involves an irreducible ontological posit, corresponding to the world's being primitively unsettled about which precise SOA obtains. Barnes and Cameron don't expand on what it is for the world to be unsettled in this way, but whatever the further details, our accounts are on a par so far as positing an irreducible kind of entity is concerned.

Moreover, the irreducible posit on their view, unlike the irreducible posit on my view, is new and unfamiliar. What exactly *is* it that is supposed to be unsettled, on their view? If it is the world, then it seems that unsettledness will involve an unfamiliar kind of property—say, *being primitively metaphysically unsettled about which precise SOA obtains*. Alternatively, if different precise SOAs correspond ultimately to different worlds, then it seems that unsettledness will involve an unfamiliar kind of entity—say, a meta-world space—having the unfamiliar property of *being primitively metaphysically unsettled about which world is actual*. Perhaps Barnes and Cameron would reject these further characterizations, but to the extent that they do not or cannot characterize unsettledness in familiar terms, it remains that this posit is not just primitive, but unfamiliar. As such, a determinable-based account has an ontological advantage over Barnes and Cameron's account, since it is less of a cost to posit the irreducibility of a familiar property than to introduce an unfamiliar primitive.

4. Closing Remarks

I've argued that my determinable-based object-level account of MI has a number of advantages over Barnes and Cameron's meta-level 'Unsettledness' account, and that my account has the resources to respond to concerns they raise against it and against Third-Way views. Along the way two more general issues have become clear. First, not all accounts of MI take MI to induce indeterminacy in propositions—in particular, mine doesn't. Second, what answer one is inclined to give to the question 'Are there indeterminate SOAs?' will depend on the details of how such SOAs are understood. I agree with Barnes and Cameron in rejecting indeterminate SOAs understood as involving unfamiliar notions such as indeterminate instantiation, or unfamiliar properties such as 'being indeterminately F.' But on my account, indeterminate SOAs involve just a pattern of ordinary instantiation of determinable and determinate properties of the sort that we already have reason to accept. That this pattern accommodates MI in an intelligible, reductive, and systematic way provides further reason to say: yes, understood as per *Determinable-based MI*, there are indeterminate SOAs.

Notes

* Thanks to David Balcarras, Elizabeth Barnes, Ross Cameron, and Benj Hellie, as well as to audiences at the 2014 PERSP Final Workshop at the University of Barcelona, the 2014 Midwest Metaphysics Conference, and Iowa State University.

1. See also Barnes 2006, Barnes and Cameron 2009, Barnes and Cameron 2011, Barnes and Williams 2011 and Barnes 2012.

2. This definition is simplified in ways that do not matter for what follows. See Wilson 2013 for a more detailed presentation of the view.

3. Some think that the seeming indeterminacy in this case can be understood in semantic terms (whereby our use of the expression 'Mount Everest' has not fixed its precise boundary, though it could in principle do so); I don't find this plausible, but in any case various special science entities (e.g., molecules, cells) are also plausibly taken to have indeterminate boundaries, for reasons having to do with the operative laws of nature as opposed to anything semantic.

4. This intuitive plausibility is supported by arguments in Yablo 1992 and Wilson 2009 according to which realization of macro-entities and their properties by 'lower-level' micro-aggregates and their properties involves the determinable/determinate relation.

5. Interestingly, and in contrast to the feather case, one might not be inclined to attribute the determinate boundary properties to Mount Everest, even in relativized fashion.

6. See Wilson (in progress) for further discussion of quantum MI.

7. Similarly for other propositions about Mount Everest, concerning, for example, where Mount Everest is located or whether a given atom is part of Mount Everest. Taking the structure of determination into account, such claims will either be true or false (or perhaps meaningless, if a needed relativization parameter fails to be filled in), not indeterminate.

8. Consider, for example, a gappy treatment of Schrödinger's cat. Here it is true that there is a cat in the box, true that the cat has a certain (quantum) determinable property corresponding to the state of superposition, false that the cat is alive, and false that the cat is dead. As such, it is false that it is indeterminate what determinate of the determinable

has—e.g., indeterminate whether the cat is alive; again, for any determinate of the determinable property at issue, it is false, not indeterminate, that the cat has that property.

9. For example, in cases of indeterminate composition, the bearer of the determinable property might be a plurality of atoms, and the determinable property would be 'potentially composing an object' (which property might be constituted by other properties of the atoms, such as proximity and strength of interaction), having determinates on which, relative to some circumstances or criteria, the plurality does compose another object, and determinates on which, relative to other circumstances or criteria, the plurality does not do so.

10. See note 8 for discussion of how gappy MI poses no problem for the law of excluded middle.

11. For example, Evan's claim that macro-object boundary indeterminacy gives rise to indeterminate identity presupposes a meta-level account, according to which if an object has an indeterminate boundary property, then it is indeterminate to which precisely boundaried object it is identical.

References

Barnes, Elizabeth. 2006. *Conceptual Room for Ontic Vagueness*. Ph.D. thesis, University of St. Andrews.

———. 2010. "Ontic Vagueness: A Guide for the Perplexed." *Nouˆs* 44: 601–627.

———. 2012. "Emergence and Fundamentality." *Mind* 121: 873–901.

Barnes, Elizabeth and Ross Cameron. 2009. "The Open Future: Bivalence, Determinism and Ontology." *Philosophical Studies* 146: 291–309.

Barnes, Elizabeth and Ross P. Cameron. 2011. "Back to the Open Future." *Philosophical Perspectives* 25: 1–26.

Barnes, Elizabeth and J.R.G. Williams. 2011. "A Theory of Metaphysical Indeterminacy". In Karen Bennett and Dean W. Zimmerman (eds.), *Oxford Studies in Metaphysics, volume 6*, 103–148. Oxford: Oxford University Press.

Bokulich, Alisa. 2014. "Metaphysical Indeterminacy, Properties, and Quantum Theory." *Res Philosophica* 91: 449–475.

Browne, Malcolm W. August 21, 1990. 'New Direction in Physics: Back in Time'. *The New York Times*.

Calosi, Claudio and Jessica Wilson. In progress. "Quantum Metaphysical Indeterminacy".

Darby, George. 2010. "Quantum Mechanics and Metaphysical Indeterminacy." *Australasian Journal of Philosophy* 88: 227–245.

Evans, Gareth. 1983. "Can There Be Vague Objects?" *Analysis* 38: 208.

Johnsgard, Paul. 1997. *The Hummingbirds of North America*. Washington, DC: Smithsonian Institution Press.

Skow, Bradford. 2010. "Deep Metaphysical Indeterminacy." *Philosophical Quarterly* 60: 851–858.

Todd, Patrick. Forthcoming. "Future Contingents Are All False! On Behalf of a Russellian Open Future." *Mind*.

Tye, Michael. 1996. "Fuzzy Boundaries and the Problem of the Many." *Philosophical Studies* 81: 215–225.

Wilson, Jessica M. 2009. "Determination, Realization, and Mental Causation." *Philosophical Studies* 145: 149–169.

———. 2012. "Fundamental Determinables." *Philosophers' Imprint* 1–17.

———. 2013. "A Determinable-Based Account of Metaphysical Indeterminacy." *Inquiry* 56: 359–385.

Wolff, Johanna. 2015. "Spin as a Determinable." *Topoi* 34: 379–386.

Yablo, Stephen. 1992. "Mental Causation." *The Philosophical Review* 101: 245–280.

CHAPTER 8

Are There Indeterminate States of Affairs? No[1]

ELIZABETH BARNES AND ROSS CAMERON

1. Two Views on Worldly Indeterminacy

Most propositions are such that their truth or falsity demands something of reality.[2] Perhaps not all do so. Perhaps the truth-teller—'This sentence is true'—expresses a proposition, and this proposition has a truth-value that is untethered to reality in the sense that it is not determined as a result of what states of affairs obtain or fail to obtain.[3] Perhaps necessary truths are similarly untethered to reality.[4] But in normal cases at least, the truth of a proposition demands of the world that it be a certain way, and its falsity demands of the world that it be some other way. Truth and falsity of propositions imposes worldly requirements.

We will here characterise such requirements as the obtaining, or failing to obtain, of certain states of affairs. But we do not intend by this talk to commit ourselves to an ontology like that of David Armstrong,[5] whereby in addition to particulars and properties and relations there are things—states of affairs—that essentially have those particulars and properties and relations as constituents and which, necessarily, exist if and only if the relevant particulars have the relevant properties and stand in the relevant relations. We will speak of the truth of <A is F>, e.g., as demanding of the world that the state of affairs of A being F obtain, but while this demand *might* amount to the demand that a certain Armstrongian state of affairs exist, the demand might simply be that A and F- ness exist, and that A be F, or even simply that A exist and that A be F. What we go on to say using 'states of affairs' talk should be acceptable, suitably translated, to those who favour a more austere ontology than Armstrong's.

(Thus the question that titles this paper should remain open to you even if you don't accept anything like Armstrong's ontology.)

If truth and falsity were all we had to worry about, a simple story is available to us. Every proposition, by its very nature, yields four sets of states of affairs: those whose obtaining is demanded by its truth, those whose non-obtaining is demanded by its truth, those whose obtaining is demanded by its falsity, and those whose non-obtaining is demanded by its falsity.[6]

The world consists of certain states of affairs that obtain, and thus it is settled what is true or false.

But what of cases where it is *indeterminate* whether a proposition is true or false? For some theorists, acknowledging indeterminacy will not drive them from the simple story just presented. The defender or a certain type of linguistic theory of indeterminacy will say that *propositions* are not indeterminate, it is *sentences* that are indeterminate, and that is a matter of there being no unique proposition that the sentence expresses, due to imprecision in our linguistic practices.[7]

Once we have actually settled on a particular proposition, this theorist will insist, the simple story applies. Others[8] see indeterminacy as an epistemic phenomenon: indeterminacy is a matter of our in-principle ignorance (due to a particular kind of reason) as to what proposition is expressed by a sentence, or perhaps even to the truth-conditions of the proposition expressed. Still, the simple story is fine, even though we might not even in principle be able to know *what* four sets of states of affairs are determined by some particular sentence.

But what if there is genuine worldly indeterminacy? By worldly indeterminacy we mean indeterminacy that remains even once we've specified exactly what proposition it is we're asking about, and which is a matter of how reality itself is, not simply a matter of how we know it to be.[9]

For example, consider Peter van Inwagen's view on when composition occurs: that is, when a collection of objects make up some further object. That this sometimes occurs, thinks van Inwagen, is undeniable, for we know that we ourselves exist and are made out of parts such as our brain, heart, cells, etc. But that it always occurs—that *any* collection of objects composes some further thing that has them as parts—is, thinks van Inwagen, implausible: there is, he thinks, no object that is made out of Obama's left thumb, the Eiffel tower and an atom in the sun. So just what has to happen for some things to compose some further thing? Van Inwagen answers: those things have to make up a *life*.[10]

But it can be indeterminate whether some things make up a life. There is no last picosecond at which someone is alive: death is a *process*, and there will be moments at which it is unsettled whether the living being remains. Likewise, it's not settled exactly which objects are involved in making up the living thing that is me: if a hair on my head is in the process of falling out, is that hair involved in my makeup? Van Inwagen embraces the unsettledness and accepts that composition can be indeterminate: that there will be cases where it is simply unsettled whether some things compose some further thing. And this is a matter of how the world itself is. It's not that we haven't decided what we mean by 'composition', or 'thing', and it's not that there is some unknowable compositional fact; it's that reality itself simply does not settle the issue.

Does the presence of such indeterminacy threaten the simple picture? We will describe two views: the *Unsettledness View* holds on to the simple picture in the face of worldly indeterminacy (hereafter, simply 'indeterminacy'), whilst the *Third-Way View* takes indeterminacy to mandate rejection of the simple picture.

1.1. The Unsettledness View

The simple view is right: propositions make demands on the world for their truth and their falsity. Indeterminacy is a matter of it being indeterminate *which* of those demands are met. For any proposition P, there is indeed the set, S1, of states of affairs whose obtaining is demanded by the truth of P; the set, S2, of states of affairs whose non-obtaining is demanded by the truth of P; and the sets, S3 and S4, whose obtaining and non-obtaining respectively is demanded by the falsity of P. When it is indeterminate whether some proposition P is true, that is a matter of it being indeterminate what states of affairs obtain: the world itself doesn't settle whether or not the members of S1 obtain and the members or S2 fail to obtain or, on the other hand, that the members of S3 obtain and the members of S4 fail to obtain. One or other of those is the case—either the demands for P's truth are met or the demands for P's falsity are met—but the world simply does not settle which, because it does not settle which states of affairs obtain. Thus, it is indeterminate whether the demands for P's truth or P's falsity are met, and thus it is indeterminate whether or not P is true.

The Unsettledness View sees indeterminacy entering the world at the level of what states of affairs obtain or fail to obtain. As a result, the believer in this view need have no disagreement with someone who refuses to countenance worldly indeterminacy as to what states of affairs might exist or the *nature* of these states of affairs. The believer in the Unsettledness View and the epistemicist can agree that every possible state of affairs is a perfectly normal state of some ordinary things instantiating some familiar properties and standing in familiar relations. Their disagreement is not about what states of affairs could exist, or about the nature of such things; it is about whether the world can fail to settle which states obtain. Thus in the Unsettledness View, *there are no indeterminate states of affairs*. Indeterminacy is a matter of unsettledness as to what states obtain, not a matter of the obtaining of a distinctive kind of state.

The believer in the Unsettledness View answers the question that titles this paper: no.

The Third-Way View, by contrast, sees no indeterminacy in what states of affairs obtain or fail to obtain, and rather thinks that indeterminacy arises because of the obtaining of a certain special kind of state of affairs—an indeterminate state.

1.2. The Third-Way View

The simple story is too simple. Propositions by their very nature determine *six* sets of states of affairs: the two sets of states whose obtaining and non-obtaining respectively is demanded by the truth of the proposition, the two sets of states whose obtaining and non-obtaining respectively is demanded by the falsity of the proposition, and the two sets of states whose obtaining and non-obtaining respectively is demanded by the proposition's being indeterminate. The world entirely settles what states of affairs obtain, and thus it settles what propositions are true, what ones are false, and what ones are indeterminate.

On the Third-Way View, as well as propositions making demands on the world for their truth, and for their falsity, propositions also make specific demands on the world for their indeterminacy. The defender of the Third-Way View is increasing the stock of possible states of affairs she countenances: she disagrees with the defender of the Unsettledness View and the epistemicist that the only states of affairs that might obtain are those of ordinary objects instantiating familiar properties and standing in familiar relations. Those ordinary states of affairs might be what are relevant to the demands of truth and falsity, but indeterminacy demands the obtaining of a special new kind of state of affairs: perhaps the state of an object *indeterminately instantiating* a familiar property, or perhaps the state of an object instantiating the *non-familiar* property of *being indeterminately F*. Either way, the indeterminacy is part of the very nature of the state of affairs. Thus on the Third-Way View, *there are indeterminate states of affairs*. The believer in the Third-Way View answers the question that titles this paper: yes.

2. Benefits of the Unsettledness View

We accept the Unsettledness View. Indeterminacy is not a matter of the obtaining of some special states of affairs, it is a matter of the world not settling which of the familiar states of affairs happen to obtain. Here are some motivations for the Unsettledness View.

The Unsettledness View coheres with the intuitive thought that indeterminacy is a matter of unsettledness between two options, rather than the introduction of a third option. If it is indeterminate whether, for example, some things, the Xs, compose an extra object, then intuitively this is a matter of it being unsettled which of two options—there being some thing composed of the Xs, or there being no such thing—obtains. Those two options, intuitively, are exhaustive: either the Xs compose some thing or they do not, there is no other option. The phenomenon of indeterminacy is unsettledness as to which of the two exhaustive options obtains. The Unsettledness View secures this thought. When P is indeterminate, either the demands for the truth of P are met, or the demands for the falsity of P are met. It is simply unsettled which. The Third-Way View, by contrast, responds to the phenomenon of indeterminacy by introducing a third option. As well as recognising that the Xs could compose some thing or fail to compose any thing, the defender of the Third-Way View thinks the Xs could . . . be somewhere in between: that there is some kind of shadowy half-composition that the Xs can be in.[11] She sees a distinct way for the Xs to be that is not amongst the states we would accept prior to our theorising about indeterminacy, whereas the Unsettledness View is conservative about what states there could be, and sees indeterminacy arising simply in what states obtain.

We think the Third-Way View misdescribes the phenomenon of indeterminacy. We accept worldly indeterminacy because we see cases where things don't seem quite one way, or quite the other. Each option has some pull—something is speaking to P's being the case, and something is speaking to P's not being the case—but they can't both obtain, as the states are exclusive. When two options both seem good to some extent, and our problem arises because we can't say both, how does it help to just introduce a third option? The motivating idea is that the world is unsettled between two states: there are two options but reality is not so simple as to have settled on one. How have we captured that motivating thought by introducing a third option, and saying that the world is absolutely settled that this third option obtains?

A second benefit of the Unsettledness View is that it is a metaphysics that sits nicely with classical logic and semantics.[12] In particular, it does not mandate a rejection of bivalence. The defender of the Unsettledness View accepts the simple story: propositions make demands on reality for their truth, and for their falsity. And she accepts that one of those demands is met, for every proposition. Thus, every proposition is either true or false. Of course, sometimes it is indeterminate *which* demand is met, and thus it is indeterminate *whether* some proposition is true or false. But bivalence is upheld: either P is true, or it is false (there is no other option), but it is sometimes indeterminate *which*. To connect this to the previous point: the Unsettledness View upholds the intuitive idea that there are two, exhaustive and exclusive, truth-values—truth and falsity—but that some propositions cannot neatly be assigned either. It takes this unsettledness between *two* truth-values at face value rather than attempting to account for the phenomenon by introducing a third valence, and saying that propositions can now neatly be classified as having one of these three truth-values. This, we think, is to the Unsettledness

View's advantage: having three neat boxes to divide propositions amongst does not capture the target phenomenon of it being unsettled in to which of two boxes to place them.[13]

The Third-Way View, by contrast, suggests (even if it does not outright mandate) a rejection of bivalence. After all, the defender of the Third-Way View holds that, in the presence of indeterminacy, neither the demands for P's truth nor the demands for P's falsity are met. What is met is a third, distinct demand: the demands for its indeterminacy. Indeterminacy as to P, on this way of thinking, seems to be incompatible with both the truth and the falsity of P. It is a genuinely third state, the obtaining of which excludes the other two. The natural thing to say, on this view, is that when P is indeterminate, it has a third truth-value, or lacks a truth-value, but that it is neither true nor false, and thus we get a failure of bivalence.

We say that rejection of bivalence is a natural thing to say given the Third-Way View, not that it is mandated. The argument from the Third-Way View to the failure of bivalence relies on the principle that if the demands for P's truth/falsity are not met by the world, then P is not true/false. We think that it is a pretty good principle—if P, by its very nature, demands of the world that it be a certain way in order for P to be true, then how could the world fail to be that way and P be true nonetheless? But it is open to the defender of the Third-Way View to deny this plausible principle, and thus hold on to bivalence. Patrick Greenough, for example, suggests that when P is determinately true/false, that is a matter of P having a truthmaker/falsemaker in reality, but when it is indeterminate whether P, that is a matter of P being either true or false but its truth-value being untethered to anything worldly: it will be true/false, but have no truthmaker/falsemaker.[14] Indeterminacy, on this view, is having a truth-value without the world playing a role in determining that truth-value.

The defender of the Third-Way View could follow Greenough and say that when P's indeterminacy conditions are met, P is nevertheless either true or false, despite the demands for P's truth not being met and the demands for P's falsity not being met. Thus, they secure bivalence: P is either true or false, but it is not made so by the obtaining of states of affairs that determine, through their nature, that truth-value. But either way, the defender of the Third-Way View faces a cost that the defender of the Unsettledness View does not: either she must reject bivalence, or she must reject the plausible link between truth-value and the world meeting the demands for that truth-value.

A third benefit accruing to the Unsettledness View is that it is entirely non-committal with respect to one's broader metaphysics. You can accept any account you like as to what states potentially make up the world. The Unsettledness View will not force you to alter that account; it will simply ask you to accept that it can be unsettled which states obtain. You can take whatever metaphysical story you like—the world consists of Armstrongian states of affairs;

of atoms in the void; of ideas in the mind of God; etc.—the Unsettledness View will be compatible with that metaphysics: it simply says that it is indeterminate *which* states involving those things obtain. The Third-Way View, by contrast, demands a metaphysics that allows for the special states of affairs associated with indeterminacy. Not any metaphysics will do, so the Third-Way View is restrictive in a way the Unsettledness View is not.[15]

Relatedly, the Third-Way View forces you to take a stand on an issue you might have expected to be able to remain neutral on just by accepting indeterminacy, concerning the relationship between a proposition's demands for its truth and its demands for its falsity. There is sometimes a substantive metaphysical debate to be had as to whether the demands for P's falsity amount simply to the demand that the demands for P's truth *fail* to be met, or whether P's falsity makes some positive demand on the world. Consider, for example, an existential proposition such as <There are dogs>. The truth of this proposition demands of the world that there be dogs. But what does its falsity demand? There are two options. We could say that its falsity makes a merely negative demand, that the demands for truth fail to be met: that is, that there *not* be any dogs. Or we could say that its falsity makes a positive demand, that there be something whose existence is incompatible with the existence of dogs—a totality state, such as one that says that all the non-dog-involving states are all the states that obtain.[16]

The Unsettledness View is entirely neutral on this metaphysical question. One can accept the former answer and say that it is indeterminate whether the demand that there are dogs be met, or one can accept the latter answer and say that it is indeterminate whether the demand that there are dogs be met or whether the demand that there be such-and-such a totality state be met. Thus, the Unsettledness View is neutral on this metaphysical issue concerning the demands made on reality by the falsity of existential propositions. Rightly so, we think, since this issue does not appear to have anything to do with indeterminacy. The Third-Way View, by contrast, cannot accept the merely negative characterisation of the falsity demands—not, at least, without simply ruling out the possibility of indeterminacy with respect to that issue. For suppose that the falsity of <There are dogs> demands simply that the demands for its truth fail to be met: in other words, that there be no dogs. The Third-Way View says that in cases of indeterminacy with respect to P, the demands for P's truth fail to be met. That is the whole point of the Third-Way View: indeterminacy arises when the demands for truth and falsity are not met, and rather the demands for this third state are met. In meeting the indeterminacy demands, the world thereby fails to meet the truth demands. But if the demands for falsity are simply that the demands for truth fail to be met, then the Third-Way View has it that meeting the indeterminacy demands is already to meet the demands for falsity. Doing what it takes to make P indeterminate, then, is also to do what it takes to make P false, if P's falsity demands are just that its truth demands go unmet. Now, we cannot complain about the result that P is both indeterminate and false, for on our own view indeterminacy does not exclude either truth or falsity, and we take that to be a virtue of the view. But remember that on the Third-Way View, it is perfectly settled what states of affairs obtain. When P is indeterminate, it is settled that the states demanded by the truth of P fail to obtain and that the states demanded by P's indeterminacy do obtain. Thus, it is not simply that P would be indeterminate and false, but that it would be indeterminate and settledly false, and surely *that* is impossible. Thus, the Third-Way View simply cannot countenance indeterminacy in cases where the demands for falsity are simply that the demands for truth fail to be met[17], and so it is less neutral than the Unsettledness View, to the latter's advantage, we think.

3. Wilson's Third-Way View

We will end by looking at a particularly interesting version of the Third-Way View: Jessica Wilson's account of indeterminate states of affairs as the instantiating of a determinable without any instantiation of an associated determinate.[18]

Orthodoxy has it that to have a particular determinable property, you must also have one of its associated determinates. So if x is coloured, it must also be red, or blue, or green, or etc. And if it is red, it must also be scarlet, or crimson, or vermilion, or etc. And if it is scarlet, it must also be . . . and so on, down to the most specific determinates that are not determinables of any further determinates. Wilson argues, however, that indeterminacy is a lack of any of the specific determinates at some level being instantiated. So, for example, suppose that it is determinate that Ball is red, but indeterminate just what shade of red it is. That is a matter of Ball instantiating the determinable property of being red but not instantiating any further determinate of redness: so Ball fails to instantiate being scarlet, or being crimson, or being vermilion, etc. There is some intuitive pull to Wilson's account. We get the world settling that Ball is red, by the fact that Ball instantiates the property of redness, but that it leaves it unsettled just what shade of red Ball is by simply lacking any relevant ontology to make it true that Ball is one shade rather than another. However, we think that the view should ultimately be rejected.

Before we say why we reject Wilson's view, we will concede that there are two big advantages to Wilson's Third-Way View over our own Unsettledness View, one conceptual and one metaphysical, and both a result of the fact that our own view is thoroughly non-reductive concerning indeterminacy. The conceptual advantage is this: nobody who understands the machinery of determinates and determinable can fail to understand Wilson when she says that the world is metaphysically indeterminate. She has told you exactly what that means: it is for a certain kind of property to be instantiated without a certain other kind of property to be instantiated. If you understand what she means by such properties—if you grasp the determinate/determinable distinction— then there is simply no room for not understanding worldly indeterminacy. Our own account, by contrast, makes ineliminable appeal to the notion of indeterminacy when we tell you how the world is. When P is indeterminate, we tell you that either the demands for P's truth or the demands for P's falsity are met, it is simply indeterminate which. Someone who is sceptical about the very idea of worldly indeterminacy is of course not going to be helped by this. That's fine. We think that indeterminacy is like modality: notions which we need to adequately characterise the world, and which don't admit of further elucidation in simpler terms, and the only hope we can have of convincing the sceptic about indeterminacy or modal notions is to convince them that their account of the world is impoverished. But of course, it is an advantage to be able to explain an otherwise potentially puzzling notion, and Wilson's account promises to do this for indeterminacy, just as Lewis's vast ontology promises to do for the modal notions.[19] Of course, in each case, the question is whether the advantage is worth the costs, to which we will return.

The metaphysical advantage to Wilson's view is related. Just as we see indeterminacy as conceptually basic, so do we see the phenomenon of inde-terminacy as part of the fundamental bedrock of reality. In Siderian terms, indeterminacy carves the world at its joints, on our view.[20]

Wilson, by contrast, offers an ontological reduction of indeterminacy: *what it is* to be indeterminate is for a certain determinable to be had without a unique associated determinate being had. In giving us a *what it is* claim, she thereby avoids the need to think of reality as having primitive structure corresponding to indeterminacy. This is an advantage over our view, just as Lewis's modal realism provides an advantage over views that see the world as a fundamentally modal place.

It is important to note, however, that these issues are independent of the issue as to whether the Unsettledness or Third-Way view of indeterminacy is correct. *Our particular version* of the Unsettledness View is non-reductionist, and *Wilson's particular version* of the Third-Way View is reductionist, but there are reductionist versions of the Unsettledness View and non-reductionist ver-sions of the Third-Way View. Consider the Third-Way View that says that when it is indeterminate whether Ball is red, there obtains the state of affairs of Ball indeterminately instantiating the property of redness. Here the notion of indeterminacy is invoked to characterise the special states of affairs associated with something's being indeterminate. If the story ends there, this account is as thoroughly non-reductionist as our own. Wilson gains the benefits she does not because she is a believer in the Third-Way View, but because of the particular account she offers of the states of affairs associated with indeter-minacy. Similarly, the Unsettledness View says that it is indeterminate what ordinary states of affairs obtain. *Our* view is non-reductionist because we end the story there. But nothing about the Unsettledness View *per se* prevents a further reductive account of indeterminacy being given. We just happen not to find any such reduction plausible, and thus accept a non-reductive story. So whether or not one obtains these advantages associated with giving a reductive account of indeterminacy is independent of the issue driving this chapter: whether there are indeterminate states of affairs.

Nevertheless, Wilson's account secures those benefits and our own does not. However, we think that these advantages can only be secured by Wilson at a cost that is not worth paying. Notice that in order for these benefits to be secured, Wilson's account has to apply in all cases of worldly indeterminacy. If there is a single case of indeterminacy that does not fit this model, then the account cannot be telling us *what it is* for something to be indeterminate, and at best it is an account of what happens to be going on in the world in specific cases of indeterminacy. But while Wilson's account has some intuitive plausibility in the above case of a thing being red but no determinate shade of red, we think it is implausible to hold that it applies in all potential cases of worldly indeterminacy. And hence the version of the view that secures the benefits just discussed is unduly restrictive as to what cases of indeterminacy can arise.

Consider, for example, cases of indeterminate existence. If it is indeterminate whether A exists, on our view that is because there are two potential states of affairs—the state of A existing, and the state of A not existing—and the world has not settled which state obtains. What is Wilson's account? This certainly does not look like a case that fits into the determinate/determinable model, for there is no determinable that has existence and non-existence as determinates. And even if there were, it would surely be wrong to say that the indeterminacy of A's existence consists in its having this determinable—*having some state of being*, say—without having either of those determinates. For in saying that A has the determinable, we are *presupposing* the existence of A, and it's not even settled that there *is* such a thing.

Likewise with indeterminate identity (e.g. if it is indeterminate whether A=B), on our view that is a matter of the world not settling which of two states obtain: the state that there is one thing, A/B, and the state that there are two things, A and B. What is Wilson's account? Again, identity and distinctness don't look like determinates of some more general determinable in the way that scarlet and crimson are determinates of red. We have argued elsewhere that the open future is a case of worldly indeterminacy. That if it is open whether or not there will be a space battle tomorrow, then this is a matter of the world not being settled between two competing future states of affairs, one in which the space battle happens and one in which it doesn't.[21]

Again, it's not clear how this can be handled by Wilson's account. Are we meant to hold that there is a determinable *having a future* that the world has, without having any determinate of the form *having such-and-such a particular future*? To say this just doesn't seem to be using our familiar notion of determinates and determinables; and so it is far from obvious that the account really would have the advantages claimed for it. Thus, we think Wilson's particular version of the Third-Way View isn't actually so advantageous after all, which is why we hold the Unsettledness View and say: there are no indeterminate states of affairs.

Notes

1. Thanks to Trenton Merricks, Jason Turner, Robbie Williams, and Jessica Wilson for helpful discussion.
2. Cf. Rayo (2007).
3. See Sorensen (2001) and Greenough (2011) for discussion.
4. Cameron (2010).
5. Armstrong (1997).
6. We can talk of sets here because we're thinking of the demands in terms of the (non-) existence of certain *things*—states of affairs—that can be the members of these sets. If you don't want to reify the demands in that manner, just think instead of a proposition P as generating four lists: the list of ways the world is demanded to be if P is true, the list of ways the world is demanded not to be if P is true, etc.

    And of course, some of these sets might be empty. Do not understand the states demanded by the truth of p, as the states that, necessarily, obtain if P is true. The truth of 'Ball is red' perhaps demands that the state of Ball being red obtains, but not that the state of 2 + 2 being 4 obtains, even though the latter state must obtain if it is true that Ball is red (since it must obtain, *simpliciter*). See Rayo (2007) for discussion.
7. See, *inter alia*, Fine (1975).
8. The classic defense being Williamson (1994).
9. See Barnes (2010).
10. Van Inwagen (1990).
11. See Hawley (2002) for relevant discussion.
12. See especially Barnes and Williams (2011).
13. See Barnes (2010) in particular for this complaint. Also Barnes and Williams (2011). Cf. Wright (2003).
14. Greenough (2008).
15. See Barnes (2010).
16. As in, e.g., Armstrong (1997, Ch. 13; 2004, Ch. 6).
17. See Cameron (2015, Ch. 5) for discussion.
18. Wilson (2013).
19. Lewis (1986).
20. Sider (2013). In more Finean terms: on our view, there are fundamental facts of the form, 'It is indeterminate whether . . .'. See Fine (2013). See Cameron (2015: Ch. 3) for discussion of the Finean versus the Siderian view, and Cameron (2015: Ch. 5) for discussion of metaphysical indeterminacy seen through the Finean lens.
21. Barnes and Cameron (2009, 2011).

References

Armstrong, D.M. 1997. *A World of States of Affairs*. Cambridge: Cambridge University Press.
———. 2004. *Truth and Truthmakers*. Cambridge: Cambridge University Press.
Barnes, Elizabeth. 2010. "Ontic Vagueness: A Guide for the Perplexed." *Noûs* 44 (4): 607–627.
Barnes, Elizabeth and Ross Cameron. 2009. "The Open Future: Bivalence, Determinism and Ontology." *Philosophical Studies* 146 (2): 291–309.

———. 2011. "Back to the Open Future". *Philosophical Perspectives: Metaphysics* 25: 1–26.

Barnes, Elizabeth and J.R.G.W. Williams. 2011. "A Theory of Metaphysical Indeterminacy." *Oxford Studies in Metaphysics* 6: 103–148.

Cameron, Ross. 2010. "Necessity and Triviality." *The Australasian Journal of Philosophy* 88 (3): 401–415.

———. 2015. *The Moving Spotlight: An Essay on Time and Ontology*. Oxford: Oxford University Press.

Fine, Kit. 1975. "Vagueness, Truth and Logic." *Synthese* 54: 235–259.

———. 2013. "Fundamental Truth and Fundamental Terms." *Philosophy and Phenomenological Research* 87 (3): 725–732.

Greenough, Patrick. 2008. "Indeterminate Truth". In Peter French (ed.), *Truth and Its Deformities, Midwest Studies in Philosophy* 32 (1): 213–241.

———. 2011. "Truthmaker Gaps and the No-No Paradox." *Philosophy and Phenomenological Research* 82 (3): 547–563.

Hawley, Katherine. 2002. "Vagueness and Existence." *Proceedings of the Aristotelian Society* 102 (1): 125–140.

Rayo, Agustin. 2007. "Ontological Commitment." *Philosophy Compass* 2 (3): 428–444.

Sider, Theodore. 2013. *Writing the Book of the World*. Oxford: Oxford University Press.

Sorensen, Roy. 2001. *Vagueness and Contradiction*. Oxford: Oxford University Press.

van Inwagen, Peter. 1990. *Material Beings*. Ithaca, NY: Cornell University Press.

Williamson, Timothy. 1994. *Vagueness*. London: Routledge.

Wilson, Jessica. 2013. "A Determinable-Based Account of Metaphysical Indeterminacy." *Inquiry* 56 (4): 359–385.

Wright, Crispin. 2003. "Vagueness: A Fifth Column Approach". In J.C. Beall (ed.), *Liars and Heaps: New Essays on Paradox*, 84–105. Oxford: Oxford University Press.

PART V

Do Ordinary Objects Exist?

CHAPTER 9

Do Ordinary Objects Exist? No*

TRENTON MERRICKS

1. Three Bad Arguments

Consider a pair of gloves. Name the left glove 'Lefty' and the right glove 'Righty'. Lefty and Righty are ordinary objects; thus, we have the ordinary word 'glove', which applies to Lefty and also applies to Righty. Perhaps Lefty and Righty compose an object. That is, perhaps there is an object that has exactly Lefty and Righty (and their parts) as its parts. Name that object 'Pair'. Pair seems to be an ordinary object too; after all, we have the ordinary expression 'pair of gloves', which seems to apply to Pair.

Here is an argument for the existence of Pair.

ARGUMENT ONE: Yesterday I was out in the cold, and my hands stayed warm. Lefty did not cause that—Lefty kept only my left hand warm. And Righty did not cause that—Righty kept only my right hand warm. But surely something caused my hands—both of them—to stay warm. Pair is the obvious candidate. Nothing can keep both my hands warm unless it exists. So Pair exists.

Argument One is a bad argument. This is because even if Pair does not exist—that is, even if Lefty and Righty compose nothing at all—we can still give a full causal account of both hands being kept warm despite the frosty temperature. Here it is: Lefty kept the left hand warm and Righty kept the right hand warm.

This account does not say that any one thing kept both hands warm, but rather that two things did: Lefty and Righty, working in concert, kept both hands warm, together causing what neither causes on its own. This is no more mysterious than your and my carrying a couch, a couch that neither you nor I alone could carry. And this no more gives us a good reason to think that Pair exists than does your and my carrying the couch give us a good reason to think that there is a big two-headed object made up partly of me and partly of you.

Note that, for all I have said so far, Pair might have caused both hands to stay warm, as did Lefty and Righty. (And, for all I have said so far, a two-headed object might have carried the couch, as did you and I.) So Pair might exist. So Argument One—like lots of bad arguments—might happen to have a true conclusion. My only point here—at this stage—is that Argument One is a bad argument because your hands' remaining warm while you are out in the cold is itself not a good reason to conclude that Pair exists, not even if there must be a causal explanation of your hands' remaining warm.

Here is a second argument for the existence of Pair.

ARGUMENT TWO: I put Lefty and Righty on a scale and the scale registered a weight of twelve ounces. But Lefty weighs in at a mere six ounces. The same goes for Righty. So neither Lefty nor Righty caused the scale to register twelve ounces. But surely something caused the scale to register twelve ounces. Pair is the obvious candidate. Only existing things can cause a scale to register a weight. So Pair exists.

Argument Two is a bad argument. This is because even if Pair does not exist, we can still fully causally account for the scale's registering twelve ounces: Lefty and Righty jointly cause the scale to register twelve ounces.

Working in concert, Lefty and Righty did together that which neither could do on its own, cause the scale to register twelve ounces. This is no more mysterious than you and me, perched together on a scale, causing it to register over three hundred pounds, even if neither of us weighs anything near three hundred pounds. And Lefty and Righty's doing this together no more gives us a reason to believe that Pair exists than does our squeezing onto the scale together give us a reason to believe that there is a big three-hundred-pound-plus object with its four feet planted on the scale.

For all I have said so far, Pair might have caused the scale to register twelve ounces, as did Lefty and Righty. (And a two-headed object composed of you and me might have caused the scale to register over three hundred pounds, as did you and I.) No matter. For now, what does matter is that when it comes to registering a weight on a scale, Pair would cause nothing new, nothing that has not already been caused by Lefty and Righty working in concert. That is why Argument Two is a bad argument.

Let us consider one more argument for the existence of Pair:

ARGUMENT THREE: I seem to see Pair. So do you—just look! Only existing things can cause visual experiences. So Pair exists.

Working in concert, Lefty and Righty cause a visual experience that neither could cause on its own. This is no more mysterious than is your and my jumping up and down causing a spectator to have a visual experience that neither you nor I alone could cause. And Lefty and Righty's jointly causing a visual experience as of a pair of gloves no more gives us a reason to believe that Pair exists than does our causing a visual experience as of two people leaping about give us a reason to believe that there is a single object, with four hands and two livers, leaping about.

Perhaps Pair is yet another cause of the visual experience as of a pair of gloves. (And perhaps a big two-livered object is yet another cause of the visual experience as of you and me jumping up and down.) Even so, I conclude that nothing in the visual experience of seeming to see Pair gives anyone who believes in Lefty and Righty a good reason to conclude that Pair exists. Argument Three is just as bad as Arguments One and Two.

2. No Good Ordinary Reasons to Believe that Pair Exists

Lefty and Righty, working in concert, cause both of your hands to remain warm. If Pair exists, then—obviously—Pair causes your hands to remain warm in all those situations in which Lefty and Righty cause your hands to remain warm. And—equally obviously—there is no situation in which Pair causes your hands to remain warm, but your hands are not also caused to remain warm by Lefty and Righty, working together. So let us say that, when it comes to keeping hands warm, Pair is at best a *mere causal overdeterminer*. Let us say, in other words, that, when it comes to keeping hands warm, Pair is at best *wholly causally redundant*. And so it goes for any other effect that Pair might cause.

If Pair exists, Pair is a mere causal overdeterminer. Pair's being a mere causal overdeterminer is why Arguments One through Three are bad. For each of those three arguments turns on the idea that a certain effect—hands' remaining warm, the registering of twelve ounces on a scale, a certain visual sensation—should lead us to conclude that Pair causes said effect, and so exists. And each of those arguments is bad because the relevant effect is fully causally explained even if Pair does not exist. That is, even if Pair does not exist, Lefty and Righty, working in concert, cause the relevant effect.[1]

It is not just Arguments One through Three that are rendered no good by Pair's being wholly causally redundant. I think that any reason for believing that Pair exists that turns on Pair's causal effects will be a bad reason. This includes reasons that turn on Pair's causal effects, but that—unlike Arguments One through Three—are not arguments at all, much less arguments that invoke the relevant effects in their premises.

To see how broadly I am using 'reason'—and to see how a reason can 'turn on' causal effects without invoking those effects in the premise of an argument—consider the following: Your experiencing your hands being kept warm directly produces in you the belief that Pair exists. This is not a case of your believing that Pair exists on the basis of an argument for Pair's existence. So it is not a case of your believing that Pair exists on the basis of Argument One. Even so, this reason for believing that Pair exists turns on Pair's causing your hands to remain warm no less than does Argument One.

I think that this reason—this experience that produces your belief in Pair—is a bad reason to believe in Pair, and is bad in much the same way that Argument One is bad. As already noted, Argument One is a bad reason for believing in Pair because even if Pair does not exist, your hands remaining warm is still fully causally explained. Analogously, your experience of your hands remaining warm is a bad reason for believing in Pair because even if Pair does not exist, you still have that experience, and it is still fully causally explained.

More generally, and only because Pair is a mere causal overdeterminer, I think that any reason for believing that Pair exists that turns on some causal effect of Pair's is a bad reason. More generally still, I think that any reason for believing that any particular wholly causally redundant physical object exists that turns on some causal effect of that object is a bad reason.

I also think that all the *ordinary* reasons to believe in the existence of any particular physical object, Pair included, turn on the causal effects of that object. To see why, pretend—just for the sake of argument and even though it is presumably impossible—that Pair exists *but has no causal effects whatsoever*. Then Pair would fail to keep any hands warm. And Pair would register no weight on a scale. And Pair would be invisible. And so on. Given what we are pretending only for the sake of argument, I think it is clear that we would have no good ordinary reasons at all for believing that Pair exists. This shows that any ordinary reasons we do have to believe that Pair exists turn on Pair's having this or that causal effect—and so are bad reasons.[2]

3. Pair Does Not Exist

There are no good ordinary reasons for believing that Pair exists. But there might be good *non*-ordinary reasons for believing that Pair exists. I assume that any such non-ordinary reasons will be 'philosophical'. That is, I assume that any such non-ordinary reasons will turn on the sorts of claims typically made, at least explicitly, only by philosophers.[3] By the same token, there might also be good philosophical reasons for denying that Pair exists. In fact, I myself have a philosophical reason for denying that Pair exists.

My philosophical reason for denying that Pair exists has two stages. The first is an 'Ockham's razor'-type principle: We should deny the existence of those alleged physical objects that would be, of necessity, wholly causally redundant, especially if we have no good ordinary reasons to believe in such objects. The second is that—as argued above—we have no good ordinary reasons to believe in physical objects that are (of necessity or otherwise) wholly causally redundant.

My philosophical reason applies to Pair only if Pair is, of necessity, wholly causally redundant. And I think it is. After all, I did not have to dream up a special scenario according to which Pair ends up being a mere causal overdeterminer, such as (for example) a scenario in which a superbeing intentionally causes whatever Pair causes. On the contrary, it seems like there is no possible scenario in which Pair is anything but a mere causal overdeterminer. Pair is *essentially* a mere causal overdeterminer. That is, Pair is, *of necessity*, wholly causally redundant.[4]

Here is one way to motivate my philosophical reason for denying that Pair exists. Imagine that some claim that a certain object O causes the water in your tea kettle to get hot. They admit that your stove causes this as well. They clarify that O overdetermines the heating of the water, and add that no part of your stove is a part of O and no part of O is a part of your stove. They also claim that O causes the rain to stay outside your house, but admit that O is thereby causally overdetermining the effect of your roof, which itself is not a part of O nor is any part of O a part of it. They add that none of this has anything to do with your stove or your roof in particular. Rather, they further add, this is all because every effect O causes is also (of necessity) caused by other things, and, moreover, none of those things is a part of O and no part of O is a part of any of them. Finally, they add that no one has any good ordinary reasons to believe in O.

First, O would be essentially a mere causal overdeterminer. Second, we have no good ordinary reasons to believe that O exists. I say that these two facts together constitute one good philosophical reason—there are others—to deny that O exists. So I do deny that O exists. And I bet you do too. But if these two facts constitute a good philosophical reason to deny that O exists, then the two parallel facts regarding Pair, defended above, constitute a good philosophical reason to deny that Pair exists. This is why I deny that Pair exists.

My philosophical reason for concluding that O does not exist could be outweighed by philosophical reasons to conclude that O does exist. Likewise, my philosophical reason for concluding that Pair does not exist could be outweighed by philosophical reasons to conclude that Pair exists. And there are some who do defend philosophical reasons for the existence of Pair.

For example, some philosophers argue for unrestricted composition, that is, for the conclusion that, for any objects whatsoever, those objects compose something. That conclusion is a philosophical reason to believe that Pair exists, since it is a philosophical reason to believe that Lefty and Righty compose something. Moreover, that philosophical reason is not touched by my above arguments that undermined ordinary reasons for believing in Pair. This is because the arguments for unrestricted composition do not turn on the alleged causal effects of composite objects.

I think that the arguments for unrestricted composition fail (see Merricks 2005). But you might disagree. Or you might offer other philosophical arguments for the existence of Pair, arguments that do not proceed by way of unrestricted composition. Similarly, my aforementioned philosophical reason to conclude that Pair does not exist could be buttressed by further philosophical reasons for that same conclusion. As we wrangle over which philosophical reasons are ultimately most persuasive, we are doing substantive metaphysics.

I think that the case can be made that the reasons for denying that Pair exists are overall the best (see Merricks 2001). You might disagree. But even if you do disagree, you would be confused if you then added that denying that Pair exists is absurd, or added that only those unMoored from common sense would claim that Pair does not exist, or added that assent to the sentence 'Pair does not exist' must be a result of language gone on holiday. On the contrary, to deny that Pair exists is simply to endorse a philosophical conclusion on an issue that all should recognise is genuinely up for grabs. All should agree that this issue of substantive metaphysics must be decided—if it is to be decided at all—by weighing the philosophical reasons that push in one direction against those that push in the other, rather than, say, by what one sees right in front of one's face.

4. Neither Does Lefty or Righty

We saw some bad arguments for the claim that Pair exists. Here are similar, and similarly bad, arguments for the claim that Lefty exists: Something must cause your left hand to remain warm in frosty weather; so Lefty exists. Something must cause the scale to register six ounces; so Lefty exists. Something must cause your visual experience of seeming to see Lefty; so Lefty exists.

Each of these brief arguments assumes that the occurrence of a certain effect—a hand's remaining warm, the registering of six ounces on a scale, a certain visual experience—gives us a good reason to conclude that Lefty exists to cause said effect. But none of these brief arguments are any better than Arguments One through Three for the existence of Pair. Each of these brief arguments is bad because the relevant effect is fully causally explained even if Lefty does not exist.

To see why I say this, suppose that if Lefty exists, Lefty is composed of a leather shell S, a wool lining L, and some thread T (T connects L to S). Then surely S, L, and T work in concert to cause your left hand to remain warm in all and only those situations in which Lefty (allegedly) also causes your left hand to remain warm. And S, L, and T jointly cause the scale to register six ounces in all and only those situations in which Lefty (allegedly) also causes the scale to register that weight. And S, L, and T jointly cause you to have a visual experience as of a left glove in all and only those situations in which Lefty (allegedly) also causes that experience.

If Lefty exists, Lefty causes a certain effect in all and only those situations in which S, L, and T cause that effect. Lefty—no less than Pair—is essentially a mere causal overdeterminer. Necessarily, Lefty is wholly causally redundant. As we saw above, this undermines certain quick arguments for the existence of Lefty. More importantly, and as we saw in Section 2, we have no good ordinary reasons to believe in the existence of a given physical object if that object is a mere causal overdeterminer. So every ordinary reason for believing in Lefty is no good. (For example, we have no good perceptual reasons for believing in Lefty, since such reasons turn on experiences that, even if Lefty does not exist, are fully causally explained by S, L, and T working in concert.)

As noted above (§3), I think that we should deny the existence of those alleged physical objects that would be, of necessity, wholly causally redundant, especially if—as with Lefty—we have no good ordinary reasons to believe in such objects. Thus, Lefty's being of necessity wholly causally redundant does not merely undermine all the ordinary reasons to believe in Lefty. It also gives us a philosophical reason to deny that Lefty exists. I conclude that Lefty does not exist. Likewise for Righty.

Even those who have their own non-ordinary and philosophical reasons for believing in Lefty should agree that there is nothing crazy or absurd in denying that Lefty exists. The claim that Lefty does not exist is not the sort of thing one might endorse only 'in the ontology room' but be unable to endorse sensibly in the ordinary business of life. Nor is the claim that Lefty does not exist refuted simply by waving S, L, and T—or even Lefty itself—in my face.

5. Neither Does S, L, or T

Even if Pair does not exist, we can still causally explain both hands remaining warm, despite the cold. For Lefty keeps the left hand warm and Righty keeps the right hand warm. Or so I said in Sections 1 and 2 above. But in the preceding section, Section 4, I argued that neither Lefty nor Righty exists. So I must conclude that neither Lefty nor Righty keeps any hand warm. So I must revise my objection to Argument One. For parallel reasons, I must also revise my objections to Arguments Two and Three, along with my reason for denying

that Pair exists, a reason that turned on Pair's being of necessity wholly causally redundant because of what Lefty and Righty jointly cause.

The most obvious revision says that S, L, and T, working in concert, keep
the left hand warm; and the shell, lining, and thread that allegedly compose
Righty keep the right hand warm. My objections to Arguments One through
Three and to the existence of Pair then proceed more or less as above. But of
course this most obvious revision cannot be the final story. For S, L, and T
(if they exist) are essentially mere overdeterminers in just the same way that
Lefty and Righty and Pair (if they exist) are essentially mere overdeterminers.
For S, L, and T each cause an effect only in those circumstances in which their
respective parts, working in concert, cause that same effect.

So my argument against Pair turns into an argument against Lefty and
against Righty, which in turn turns into an argument against S, L, T, and the
lining, shell, and thread that seem to compose Righty. Where does it end? Presumably not with the left half of S, the right half of S, the left half of L, and
so on. For if the left half of S exists, it has parts, and those parts, working in
concert, cause whatever the left half of S causes, and likewise for the right half
of S and the left half of L, and so on.

6. Two Options

A *simple* has no parts. Suppose that a particular simple has causal effects. It
might be possible for that simple to be rendered entirely causally redundant by
way of, say, a superbeing who has decided to cause whatever that simple causes
throughout the duration of that simple's existence. But none of this would be
that simple's fault. Nor would any of this suggest that that simple is, of necessity, wholly causally redundant.

In fact, it is hard to see how a simple could be, of necessity, wholly causally redundant. For a simple has no parts, so it has no parts that, working in
concert, cause exactly what it causes. Nor do I think that any simple shares its
location, of necessity, with various other simples, all of which cause exactly
what it causes. And it is surely false that in every possible situation something
or other—such as a bizarre superbeing, or an equally bizarre law of nature—
would crop up to render a given simple wholly causally redundant. So I conclude that if there are simples that have causal effects, those simples are not
essentially mere causal overdeterminers.

Suppose that there are simples. And consider those simples that, if Pair
exists, compose Pair. Suppose further that those simples, working in concert, cause all that Pair causes, if Pair exists. Given these suppositions—and
given that those simples are not themselves of necessity causally redundant—I
would follow the reasoning defended in this chapter 'all the way down' and
conclude that there is nothing where we think that there is a pair of gloves
besides those simples.

Maybe there are no simples. Or maybe there are simples, but simples do not cause effects, not in the sense of 'cause' in which Pair (if it exists) causes effects. Even so, there might still be some smallest physical objects that cause effects in the way that Pair (if it exists) causes effects. That is, it might be that at a certain point as we descend from Pair to Lefty to T to T's larger parts to the parts of T's larger parts, and so on, we reach a point at which the parts no longer cause effects, not even working in concert, not in the sense of 'cause' in which pairs of gloves or gloves or leather shells or wool linings are alleged to cause effects.[5]

With this in mind, suppose that if Pair exists, it has among its parts some objects $x_1 \ldots x_n$ that cause effects (in the sense of 'cause' in which Pair would cause effects). Add that $x_1 \ldots x_n$ have all and only $y_1 \ldots y_n$ as parts. And add that $y_1 \ldots y_n$ do not cause effects (not in the sense of 'cause' in which Pair would cause effects). Then we can take the above reasoning for the claim that simples would not be essentially mere causal overdeterminers and tweak it to show that $x_1 \ldots x_n$ would not be essentially mere causal overdeterminers. Then, for the sorts of reasons presented in Sections 3 through 5, I would conclude that $x_1 \ldots x_n$ are not only the 'smallest causers' but also the biggest objects located in a region that we would ordinarily think contains a pair of gloves.

7. An Objection

There might be simples that cause effects in the way that gloves cause effects. Or there might be non-simple 'smallest causers'. Those are two options. And I think that there are further options that would fit with the line of argument I have been defending against the existence of Lefty and Righty and Pair (see Merricks 2001: 115). But there is one alleged possibility that might seem to threaten the line of argument I have been defending. Here it is: First, every physical object has parts that are physical objects (so there are no physical simples). Second, for every physical object, the parts of that object, working in concert, cause exactly the same effects (in the sense of 'cause' in which gloves are alleged to cause effects) as that object itself causes.

I do not know whether this alleged possibility really is possible, and I doubt that anyone else knows either. But let us assume that this alleged possibility really is possible. And let us also assume that this possibility implies that it is possible that there are some physical objects that are essentially mere causal overdeterminers. These assumptions might seem to threaten my overall argument for the conclusion that Lefty and Righty and Pair do not exist.

But I do not think the threat is very serious. To begin to see why, recall this example from above: Imagine that some claim that there exists a certain object O that causes the water in your kettle to get hot. They admit that your stove causes this as well. They clarify that O overdetermines the heating of that water. They also claim that O causes your rugs to remain dry during a rainstorm, admitting that O is merely causally overdetermining an effect caused by your roof. They then add that, necessarily, every effect caused by O is also caused by other things, none of which is a part of O and no part of O is a part of any of those other things. They then concede that there are no good ordinary reasons to believe in O.

As noted above, I would conclude that O does not exist. For, as noted above, I think the fact that O would be essentially a mere causal overdeterminer is a good philosophical reason to deny that it exists, especially since there is no good ordinary reason to believe in O.

But now consider this alleged possibility: There is an object that is exactly like O, as just described. I do not know whether this alleged possibility really is possible. But assume that it is. Even assuming this, I still conclude that O does not actually exist. And I still say that the following principle gives us a good reason to conclude that O does not exist: We should deny the existence of those alleged physical objects that would be, of necessity, wholly causally redundant, especially if we have no good ordinary reasons to believe in such objects.

If it is possible for an object like O to exist, then this principle would lead us astray in some 'possible worlds'. So too would a principle such as 'we should deny that there are any physical objects that are, as a matter of staggering coincidence, mere overdeterminers, all of whose effects are caused by entities that are not their parts and of which they are not themselves parts'. I suppose that there are also 'possible worlds' in which a principle such as 'everything else being equal, adopt the simpler and more elegant theory' would lead us astray. And the same goes for a principle such as 'trust inductions made with regard to natural properties, but not with regard to gerrymandered properties'. So what? A principle that guides theory choice can be the right principle to follow even if it would lead us astray in some 'possible worlds'.

So I deny that the mere possibility of an object like O automatically undermines every philosophical reason to deny that O exists. In particular, I deny that that mere possibility undermines my own reason for denying that O exists. (That mere possibility does undermine those reasons that—unlike my own—rely on the claim that an object like O is impossible.) For perfectly analogous reasons, I do not think that the reason defended in this essay for denying the existence of Pair and Lefty and Righty is undermined simply by the mere possibility of there being physical objects that are, of necessity, wholly causally redundant.

Set aside mere possibility. Suppose—for the sake of argument—that the following is in fact how things really are: First, every physical object has parts. And, second, for every physical object, the parts of that object, working in concert, cause exactly the same effects (in the sense of 'cause' in which gloves are alleged to cause effects) as that object itself causes. Suppose that we even know that this is how things actually are.

I concede that, given these suppositions, we cannot say that there are absolutely no physical objects that are, of necessity, wholly causally redundant. But these suppositions do not imply that Pair or Lefty or Righty exists. In fact, even if I endorsed these suppositions, I would still deny the existence of Pair and Lefty and Righty. I would even do so for an Ockham's-razor type reason. That reason claims that we should deny *to the extent that we can* the existence of those alleged physical objects that would be, of necessity, wholly causally redundant, especially if we have no good ordinary reasons to believe in those objects. We can say that Pair and Lefty and Righty do not exist. And this is what I would say.

Defenders of Lefty and Righty and Pair might object that there is something arbitrary about wielding Ockham's razor once it is qualified with *to the extent that we can*. That is, they might object that it is arbitrary to use the razor to rule out familiar macroscopic objects while also conceding that at some point there will be smaller objects that are, of necessity, wholly causally redundant.

Their sort of reasoning aims to purchase a decrease in apparent arbitrariness with an increase in objects that are, of necessity, wholly causally redundant. I myself find it more plausible to get rid of as many such objects as we can. And this seems like the right move to me even if its cost is conceding both that we do not know how 'far down' to 'draw the line' and start admitting such objects, and also that if we did know where that line was to be drawn, it might seem arbitrary to us.

Besides, once we have a descending series of essentially wholly causally redundant objects that goes 'all the way down', I suspect that the only view that really does purchase a decrease in apparent arbitrariness says that the hierarchy of such entities goes 'all the way up' as well. This view delivers not just the existence of Lefty and Righty and Pair, but also unrestricted composition. And I say that—whatever we say about Lefty and Righty and Pair—we should reject unrestricted composition.

I say this because unrestricted composition brings serious problems in its wake, problems best avoided by rejecting unrestricted composition.[6] So I think that—given that we should reject unrestricted composition—endorsing the existence of Lefty, Righty, and Pair does not free us from the sort of arbitrariness that those who object to my 'qualified Ockham's razor' want to avoid. And as long as we have the apparent arbitrariness anyway, we might as well—at no additional cost—get rid of the essentially merely overdetermining Lefty and Righty and Pair.

Not everyone will agree. For example, some will insist that we should rid ourselves of all apparent arbitrariness here, even if that means endorsing unrestricted composition. So they will conclude that Lefty and Righty and Pair exist. Obviously enough, they have reached that conclusion not for ordinary reasons, but for philosophical ones. Again, they have reached that conclusion not because, for example, they can see Lefty and Righty and Pair, but rather because of their conviction that avoiding a certain kind of arbitrariness is a benefit that outweighs the costs of unrestricted composition. Fair enough. But, as already noted, I do not share their conviction. And, more importantly, I think that the overall philosophical reasons to deny the existence of Lefty and Righty and Pair are more compelling than the overall philosophical reasons to believe that such objects exist (see Merricks 2001).

Besides, the philosophical defense of Lefty and Righty and Pair that we have just considered rests on the following claim: It actually is the case that every physical object has parts and, for every physical object, the parts of that object, working in concert, cause exactly the same effects—in exactly the same sense of 'cause'—as that object itself causes. I granted this claim for the sake of argument, and then explained how, given this claim, I would reply to that defense of Lefty and Righty and Pair. But of course no one really knows whether this claim is true. So no one should endorse the philosophical defense of the existence of Lefty and Righty and Pair that we have just considered.

8. Conclusion

I have argued that we should deny that Lefty and Righty and Pair exist. Those arguments can be adapted to support denying the existence of a wide variety of ordinary objects, objects that—if they do exist—are essentially mere causal overdeterminers. Thus, I deny the existence of not just gloves, but also scarves (and winter accessories more generally), tables, chairs, mountains, boulders, trees, and most other ordinary objects.

Sometimes the claim that most ordinary objects do not exist is met with incredulity. But such incredulity is confused. This is because all our ordinary reasons for thinking that here is one wholly causally redundant ordinary object and here is another are no good. It turns out that what one should conclude about the existence of such objects turns on philosophical reasons, some of which push in one direction, some in the other. In this way, one's view on the existence of gloves and tables and chairs is akin to one's view on the existence of abstract objects. I think that those who deny that there are abstract objects are making a mistake. I do not, however, meet their denial with incredulity, but instead with argument (Merricks 2015).

Again, I deny the existence of most ordinary objects. But not all. For you yourself are an ordinary object. (No offense.) And so am I. And I do believe that we human beings exist. This is partly because I think that each of us has good ordinary reasons to believe in his or her own existence, reasons that would not be undermined even if we did turn out to be essentially mere causal overdeterminers. And it is partly because I deny that each of us is essentially a mere causal overdeterminer. But all that is another topic.[7]

Notes

* Well, except for the ones that do; see Section 8. Thanks to Elizabeth Barnes, Ross Cameron, Becky Stangl, Adam Tiller, and, especially, Dan Korman.

1. Section 1 never uses the word 'overdetermine'. And the points made here and below can be made without using that word; for example, replace my claims about what Pair 'overdetermines' with claims about Pair's effects being caused by Lefty and Righty, working in concert. So there is no need for us to fight about whether, for example, a whole's causing what its parts cause counts as 'real overdetermination'.

2. Two points of clarification: First, I have not indulged in skeptical hypotheses to impugn ordinary reasons for believing that Pair exists. For example, I did not trade on a possible world in which an evil demon causes your visual experience as of seeing Pair. Rather, I have impugned those ordinary reasons on the grounds that the relevant effects are actually fully causally explained by Lefty and Righty working in concert, and so fully causally explained even if Pair does not cause them.

   Second, suppose that our having the expression 'pair of gloves', or someone's wanting to receive a pair of gloves for Christmas, amounts to an ordinary reason to believe that Pair exists. I say that if—as pretended above only for the sake of argument—Pair had no causal effects whatsoever (and so was invisible, etc.), then we would all agree that those supposed ordinary reasons would not be any good. I think this shows that those reasons somehow presuppose—and so 'turn on'—Pair's having this or that causal effect.

3. I do not deny the possibility of non-philosophical non-ordinary reasons. For example, suppose that you know that God is omniscient, never lies, and has told you that Pair exists. Then you have a reason to believe that Pair exists, a reason that is both non-ordinary and non-philosophical. Moreover, since this reason does not turn on Pair's causal effects, this reason is not touched by my above arguments that undermine ordinary reasons for believing in Pair.

4. Lefty and Righty, working together, result in Pair being essentially a mere causal overdeterminer. But we should not conclude, in virtue of what Pair allegedly causes, that each of Lefty and Righty is itself essentially a mere overdeterminer, of necessity causing nothing that is not already caused by Pair. For presumably each of Lefty and Righty could exist even if Pair did not. For example, destroying Righty presumably also results in Pair's non-existence, but not in Lefty's; thus it is possible—even if Pair does exist—for Lefty to cause things that Pair does not. On the other hand, I do not suppose that Pair could exist if either Lefty or Righty failed to exist, or—more cautiously—that Pair could exist without being composed of gloves (even if those gloves are not Lefty and Righty in particular) that render Pair wholly causally redundant. (Parallel remarks apply below to, e.g., the discussion of Lefty and S, L, and T.)

5. At least since Russell (1919), some philosophers have argued that the notion of *cause* has no place in physics. Suppose they are right. Suppose further that this implies that we should not credit quarks (etc.) with causing effects. Add that some entities composed of quarks (etc.) do cause effects. Then we get the view just described in the text.

6. Here is just one: If composition is unrestricted, then there is an object composed of all and only the atoms that compose you save a single atom in your left thumb. (That object is not identical with you; you have a part, the aforementioned atom, that it lacks.) Is that object a conscious person? If it is, we have two persons in your chair: you and that object. If it is not, whether something is a conscious person can turn on whether it has an extra atom in its thumb. Either result is bad. So I deny that all and only your atoms, minus one in your left thumb, compose something. So it is false that composition is unrestricted.

7. I defend these claims about human beings in *Objects and Persons*. That book also presents the sort of arguments that are presented in this chapter, but both in more detail and also in a way that engages with the relevant literature. And that book contains further philosophical arguments against objects such as Pair and Lefty and Righty.

References

Merricks, Trenton. 2001. *Objects and Persons.* Oxford: Clarendon Press.
———. 2005. "Composition and Vagueness." *Mind* 114: 615–637.
———. 2015. *Propositions.* Oxford: Clarendon Press.
Russell, Bertrand. 1919. "On the Notion of Cause." In *Mysticism and Logic and Other Essays.* London: Longmans, Green and Co., pp. 180–208.

CHAPTER **10**

Do Ordinary Objects Exist? Yes

HELEN BEEBEE

1. Introduction

Common-sense ontology—our commitment, in our everyday talk and thought, to such entities as tigers and tables and baseballs and gloves, and perhaps even to *pairs* of gloves—serves us pretty well. Trenton Merricks argues, however, that—except in the case of conscious composite objects, which he thinks *do* exist—common-sense ontology is mistaken. There *are* no tigers or tables or baseballs or gloves; there are merely smaller things (simples or 'smallest causes'; let's call them 'particles') arranged tiger-wise, glove-wise, and so on.

Merricks's argument runs as follows. First, we have no good 'ordinary' reasons to believe in what he calls 'essentially mere causal overdeterminers'. If Pair—a pair of gloves consisting of Lefty and Righty—exists, then Pair over-determines all of its effects, because there is nothing that Pair causes that isn't *also* jointly caused by Lefty and Righty. Similarly, if Lefty exists, then Lefty overdetermines all of *its* effects, because there is nothing that Lefty causes that isn't also jointly caused by S (a leather shell), L (a lining), and T (some thread). And so on. Second, we have *philosophical* reasons to *disbelieve* in things that are essentially mere causal overdeterminers—especially if we have no good ordinary reasons to believe in them. Putting the two stages of the argument together, we get the conclusion that we have good reasons to think that no composite objects such as Pair, Lefty, Righty, S, L, T, and still smaller composite objects exist.

In §§2 and 3, I consider the two halves of Merricks's argument separately. I start, in §2, with Merricks's claim that we have no ordinary reasons to believe in Lefty and its ilk, and I argue that the main principle that Merricks appeals to in his argument is unjustified. In §3, I dispute Merricks's claim that we have good *philosophical* reasons *not* to believe in Lefty. In §4, I show briefly that even if, by the lights of my own argument, we have good ordinary reasons to believe in a two-headed couch-carrying monstrosity composed of me and Trenton, the terms of the debate are such that this is does not count against the argument. Finally, in §5, I very briefly sketch a possible answer to the 'Special Composition Question'—when do some objects (such as S, L, and T) compose a further object (such as a glove)?—that broadly respects common-sense ontology.

2. The Case against Lefty

Let's start by considering Merricks's claim that Lefty (say) is '*of necessity* wholly causally redundant' (145, emphasis added). I'm going to grant the truth of that claim: it's true that, of necessity, whatever Lefty causes (if it exists) is *also* jointly caused by other things—viz, whatever composes Lefty. But we need to be careful about what we mean by 'causally redundant'. Strictly speaking, something is causally redundant if and only if either (a) it is a redundant cause or (b) it is causally inefficacious. A redundant cause is a genuine cause—a '*bona fide*' cause, as I shall put it—but is not necessary for its effect because the effect is overdetermined by that cause and some other sufficient cause.[1] Lefty is a redundant cause: Merricks does *not* claim that Lefty, if it exists, doesn't cause anything (though that would be one way for Lefty to be causally redundant). That is, he accepts that, if Lefty exists, Lefty is just as much of a cause of my left hand's staying warm as S, L, and T are, jointly, causes of its staying warm. Lefty, then (if it exists), is a *bona fide* cause of my left hand's staying warm.

Merricks's argument that we have no ordinary grounds for believing in ordinary objects, such as gloves, depends on the claim that we have no ordinary grounds for believing in objects that are (of necessity or otherwise) wholly causally redundant. But, since he accepts that gloves, if they exist, are redundant causes rather than not causes at all, I think we can safely say that he is committed to the following principle:

(A) If O (if it exists) is a wholly redundant cause, then we have no ordinary reasons to believe in O.

Merricks's argument for (A) runs roughly as follows. First of all, 'all the *ordinary* reasons to believe in the existence of any particular physical object . . . turn on the causal effects of that object' (138, emphasis in the original). However, 'any reason for believing that any particular wholly causally redundant physical object exists that turns on some causal effect of that object is a bad reason' (138). Why so? Well, any argument we might offer for the existence of a particular wholly causally redundant object (such as the three arguments Merricks considers and rejects) 'is bad because the relevant effect is fully causally explained even if Lefty [for example] does not exist' (140).

Putting things slightly differently, we have two candidate principles in the offing here:

(B) All the ordinary reasons to believe in the existence of object O turn on the effects which that object causes.
(C) All the ordinary reasons to believe in the existence of object O turn on the effects which that object *non-redundantly* causes.

In effect, Merricks endorses (C): if O (if it exists) is a mere *redundant* cause (perhaps just of all the events we know about, or perhaps—as in the case of Lefty—all events *simpliciter*), then we have no ordinary reasons to believe in O. Hence (A). And the alleged reason for endorsing (C) rather than (B) is that, in the case of a putative redundant cause O of some effect E, we already have a complete causal explanation for E, and hence no ordinary reason to believe in O.

The first part of my argument attempts to establish that we have no grounds for endorsing (C) rather than (B), and hence no grounds for endorsing (A) (unless, of course, we can think of some *other* grounds for endorsing (A); I'll return to this question later). The argument considers what I'll call 'standard' cases of causation—cases, that is, that do not involve what I'll call 'compositional overdetermination', and hence cases where we are simply ignoring (as we normally do) the question whether the effect is overdetermined by an ordinary object (if it exists) and its constituent particles. My basic claim will be that in standard cases, grounds for thinking that an object is a *bona fide* cause *at all* just *are* grounds for thinking that it is a *non-redundant* cause. This is not so in the case of compositional overdetermination: any grounds (if any) we might have for thinking that Lefty is a compositionally overdetermining cause, and hence a *bona fide* cause, would obviously *not* be grounds for thinking that Lefty is a non-redundant cause, since, we have agreed, Lefty, if it exists, is a wholly redundant cause. Hence consideration of standard cases gives us no grounds for preferring (C) over (B).

In standard cases, overdetermination is a pretty rare phenomenon. We have it in death-by-firing-squad and two-assassin cases; a case where I independently promise two different people that I'll be in the café at 4pm and am equally motivated to keep my promise to each of them; a case where someone takes an aspirin because they just hit their head on a cupboard door and then stubbed their toe really badly, and so on. But *most* run-of-the-mill causation doesn't involve overdetermination (aside from compositional overdetermination, of course, if composite objects exist): 'standard', that is, non-compositional, overdetermination is not *normal*. Standard cases of over-determination involve two shots of causal juice, as it were: two *independent* causes of the same effect. Compositional overdetermination, by contrast, involves just the one shot. The fact that S, L, and T jointly cause your hand to stay warm together with the fact (if it is a fact) that they compose Lefty *entails* that Lefty causes your hand to stay warm; we don't need to do some extra bit of empirical investigation to ascertain whether or not Lefty, in addition to S, L, and T, causes the hand-warming. There's no extra causal juice whose source we need to unearth.

This being so, in standard cases (but not in the case of compositional over-determination) we have to adduce empirical evidence for thinking that a given effect is overdetermined rather than non-redundantly caused. For any given event E, I am entitled to infer that *something* caused it; and indeed I may have specific evidence about what kind of thing that might be. (Victim has suspi-ciously long incisors and has a wooden stake through his heart. This licenses me to infer that there is a sufficient cause of Victim's death that involves a vampire slayer plunging a stake through his heart.) But, having identified *a* cause of the effect in question, I am not entitled to infer the existence of a *sec-ond*, overdetermining cause. That just wouldn't be *normal*. I am only entitled to infer the existence of a second, overdetermining cause if I can find evidence that there really was a second, independent causal process that also led to the effect—and I will only be able to do *that* if I can find some intermediate event that was likely to have caused the effect but was not itself on the path from our first cause to the effect. I might, for example, find that Victim also has a silver bullet lodged in his heart. Knowing what I know about vampires, I can legiti-mately conclude that a silver-bullet-firing gun—call it Gun—was involved in Victim's death, E.[2]

Suppose we find no silver bullet, or indeed any other object or event that we might reasonably believe to be non-redundantly caused by a silver-bullet-firing gun. Then manifestly we have no good reasons to believe in Gun *in addi-tion* to the existence of some vampire slayer or other who put the stake through Victim's heart. Why? Well, this might seem to be an excellent point at which to appeal to (C), the principle that all the ordinary reasons to believe in the exist-ence of object O turn on the effects which that object non-redundantly causes. Indeed, such an appeal appears to line up exactly with what I said above about our evidence for the existence of overdetermining causes such as Gun: our *only* evidence for the existence of Gun will come from events that Gun (if it exists) non-redundantly causes, such as the presence of a silver bullet in Vic-tim's heart—and we have no such evidence.

But here's the rub: in fact, (B), the principle that all the ordinary reasons to believe in the existence of object O turn on the effects which that object causes (*simpliciter*) will do just as well in this context. In standard cases (such as cases of vampire killing), we only have evidence that our purported object (in this case, Gun) is a *redundant* cause of anything (such as E) insofar as we have evidence that it is a *non-redundant* cause of something (such as the presence of the silver bullet). In the absence of the silver bullet (or similar), we have no reason whatsoever to believe that E was overdetermined, and hence no reason whatsoever to believe that it was redundantly caused—and so no reason to believe that it was redundantly caused by Gun in particular. So normal cases give us no grounds for upholding (C) rather than (B). As things stand, then, (A) lacks justification.

To sum up the basic point I've been driving at so far: Merricks says that 'any reason for believing that any particular wholly causally redundant physical object exists that turns on some causal effect of that object is a bad reason', and it is 'bad because the relevant effect is fully causally explained even if Lefty [for example] does not exist' (138, 140). My argument, in effect, has been that consideration of standard cases does not justify the first of those two claims. In standard cases, we are not considering *wholly* redundant physical objects, but physical objects (such as Gun) that are wholly redundant with respect to events we know about (such as E, in the case where there is no silver bullet or equivalent). In such cases, *there is* no known 'causal effect' of Gun that might serve as a reason, good or bad, for believing in Gun. It's true that the relevant events (*viz*, the ones we know about) are fully causally explained even if Gun does not exist; and that does indeed mean that we have no good reason to believe in Gun—but only because we thereby have no good reason to think that Gun, if it exists, is a *bona fide* cause of any of those events. By contrast, we *do* have good reasons to think that Lefty, if it exists, is a *bona fide* cause of plenty of events we know about.

Let's set (B) and (C) aside, then, and consider a slightly different path we might try to take from standard cases to the truth of (A). Here is a possible explanation you might adduce for the fact that, in the absence of the silver bullet, we have no ordinary reasons to believe in Gun:

> If Gun—if it exists—is causally redundant with respect to E and all other events we know about, then we have no ordinary reasons to believe in Gun.

Generalising, we might propose the following principle:

> (A*) If O—if it exists—is causally redundant with respect to all events we know about, then we have no ordinary reasons to believe in O.

Of course, we have good reasons to think that Gun, if it exists, is indeed causally redundant with respect to all of the events we know about, since we know of no events whose occurrence requires explaining by appeal to a silver bullet-firing gun. So, if (A*) is true, it might serve to explain why we have no ordinary reasons to believe in Gun. And (A*) certainly *looks* true.

Note that any purported entity that satisfies the antecedent of (A) will automatically satisfy the antecedent of (A*). Since Lefty, if it exists, is a mere causal overdeterminer of *everything* it causes (indeed, necessarily so), Lefty, if it exists, is *in fact* causally redundant with respect to every event *we know about*. So (A*) entails (A). So if ordinary cases give us good reasons to think that (A*) is true—and, as things stand, that looks like a plausible hypothesis—we have good reasons, based on ordinary cases, to think that (A) is true too. And, as I say, (A*) *looks* true. So, it seems, we have excellent reasons to endorse (A). This, then, would seem to provide us with the required motivation for endorsing (A).

Merricks himself does not address ordinary cases, and gives no indication one way or the other on whether or not he would endorse (A*). My point, however, is that (A) stands in need of motivation. (A*), it seems to me, would—if true—do this: (A*), as we've seen, entails (A), and (A*) itself would seem to be justified by consideration of perfectly commonplace, ordinary reasoning that connects causation and existence.

But *should* we endorse (A*)? I claim that we should not. As I said earlier, in standard cases (i.e. those not involving compositional overdetermination), when we already have one sufficient cause of an event locked in—the stake through the heart, for example—we have to adduce empirical evidence in order to have good reasons to think that the event in question was overdetermined: we need to find the silver bullet or equivalent. In the absence of our silver bullet, then, we are entitled to assume that the event in question was *not overdetermined at all*—after all, we know that standard overdetermination is rare, and we have no grounds for thinking that this is one of those rare cases. This being so, the reason why we have no grounds for believing in Gun is that we have no reason at all to think that any silver-bullet-firing gun was a cause of anything (relevant) that we know about. In other words, we should endorse the following principle instead of (A*):

(D) If we have no ordinary reasons to believe that any O-type thing is a *bona fide* cause of anything we know about, then we have no ordinary reasons to believe that O exists.

(D) works just fine for standard cases. It also explains why, in Merricks's case of the mysterious object O (which I shall henceforth call 'MO' for 'mysterious object' in order to avoid confusion), we have no ordinary reasons to believe in MO:

Imagine that some claim that a certain object [MO] causes the water in your tea kettle to get hot. They admit that your stove causes this as well.

They clarify that [MO] overdetermines the heating of the water, and add that no part of your stove is a part of [MO] and no part of [MO] is a part of your stove. They also claim that [MO] causes the rain to stay outside your house, but admit that [MO] is thereby causally overdetermining the effect of your roof, which itself is not a part of [MO] nor is any part of [MO] a part of it. They add that none of this has anything to do with your stove or your roof in particular. Rather, they further add, this is all because every effect [MO] causes is also (of necessity) caused by other things, and, moreover, none of those things is a part of [MO] and no part of [MO] is a part of any of them. They add that no one has any good ordinary reasons to believe in [MO].

(139)

Merricks's purpose in introducing this example is to motivate the claim that we have good *philosophical* reasons *not* to believe in MO; however, my purpose here is rather different. Merricks's protagonists 'add that no one has any good ordinary reasons to believe in [MO]'. And indeed they don't, if (A) is true, since MO is a mere overdeterminer (and, indeed, essentially so). But there is another perfectly good explanation for the fact that there is no good ordinary reason to believe in MO. Our protagonists tell us, in effect, that (a) there is some object, x, such that x overdetermines the boiling of the kettle and so on, and (b) that object is MO. But we have no grounds for thinking that the boiling of the kettle *is* overdetermined, and hence no reason to think that there is any additional *bona fide* cause of the boiling aside from the causes we already thought there were (turning the stove on, putting water in the kettle, and so on). It's perfectly true that *if* MO exists, then it overdetermines the boiling of the kettle (and so on); after all, MO is stipulatively defined as doing just that. But we have no grounds for thinking that *anything* overdetermines the boiling of the kettle, and hence no grounds for thinking that MO exists. So, while one *might* try to account for our lack of reasons to believe in MO by appealing to (A)—or indeed (A*)—(D) will do just as well.

So (D) licenses the conclusion that we have no grounds for believing in Gun (and indeed MO). Hence, we don't *need* to appeal to (A*) in order to get to that conclusion; hence, we have no grounds for endorsing (A*). Nonetheless, we are left with the worry that (A*) just *looks true*—even granted that it's not a principle we need to appeal to in order to explain why we have no grounds for believing in Gun (or MO). So maybe we still *do* have grounds for endorsing (A*) and—since (A*) entails (A)—grounds for endorsing (A). I'll argue that there are in fact no grounds for endorsing (A*) on, as it were, its own merits, and so there really are no grounds for endorsing (A*) and hence (A).

Imagine. There's been a recent spate of prince-turning-into-frog incidents. Most such incidents are caused by the casting of a single spell. But Merlin and Morgana have, for reasons best known to themselves, made a sworn pact: one of them will only ever cast a prince-to-frog spell if the other one does exactly the same thing. Their *modus operandi* is to fix a date and time for the casting of the spell and, having done so, each of them stops whatever they were doing at the allotted time, quickly whittles a wand (for reasons that will become clear), and casts their spell. Neither of them has ever broken the pact—and the two of them, given their strong dislike of princes, have implemented it on very many occasions indeed; there is barely a prince left to turn into a frog, in fact, so busy have they been. Imagine that we know all of this. Then we have perfectly good ordinary reasons to think that, when Merlin and Morgana both cast their spells, the transmogrification of their unfortunate target is overdetermined and hence that each spell was a *bona fide* cause of it, since we have excellent reasons to think that prince-to-frog spells are extremely reliable, and no grounds for thinking that, when two spells are cast (or perhaps just when two spells are cast simultaneously), one of the spells 'trumps' the other.[3]

Now, suppose the wizard police are investigating the latest prince-to-frog incident, E. They acquire excellent evidence that Merlin was a *bona fide* cause of this: his spell-casting (call this event SC1) was witnessed—on 1 April—by a very reliable police informant. Question: do we thereby have grounds for thinking that E was overdetermined? I say: yes, we do. We have excellent grounds for thinking that Morgana also cast a prince-to-frog spell on 1 April (call this event SC2).

Of course, we don't yet have any *object* whose existence is up for dispute—and hence no grounds for deciding between (A*) and (D).[4] So here's more of the story. Prince-to-frog spells are rather tedious because they require the use of a single-use-only wand—one that the wizard himself or herself must personally carve just prior to casting the spell. And the wand must have on it the wizard's name and the date the spell is cast, or else the spell won't work. Now, I just said that we have excellent ordinary reasons for thinking that Morgana cast a prince-to-frog spell on 1 April. Given our additional bit of information, I think we also thereby have excellent ordinary reasons for thinking that a certain kind of wand exists: one with 'Morgana, 1 April' carved on it. Let's call that wand, if it exists, Wand. Next question: given everything we now know, do we have ordinary reasons for thinking that Wand exists? I say: yes.

In that case, we have a counterexample—admittedly a somewhat far-fetched one—to (A*). Wand, if it exists, is causally redundant with respect to all events we know about. Hence, by (A*), we have no ordinary reasons to believe in Wand. But we *do* have such reasons. By contrast, we do not have a counterexample to (D): we do have ordinary reasons to believe that some Wand-type thing (a wand, that is, with 'Morgana, 1 April' carved on it) is a *bona fide* cause of something we know about, *viz*, E. So the antecedent of (D) is not satisfied.

Let's sum up where we've got to. We started with the thought that (A) lacks justification, because in normal cases we have no grounds for endorsing (C) rather than (B). I then proposed, on behalf of my opponent, a slightly different route we might explore that gets us justification for (A), via (A*). But that route fails because we have no grounds for preferring (A*) to (D), and (D) does not entail (A); indeed, the Merlin-Morgana case suggests that (A*) is false. Hence, we have no grounds for endorsing (A): we have no grounds for thinking that, since Lefty (if it exists) is a wholly redundant cause, we have no ordinary reasons for believing that Lefty exists.

Indeed, I *do* think we have ordinary reasons for thinking that Lefty exists. When my left hand warms up, I have ordinary reasons for thinking that this was caused by a cosy glove currently surrounding my left hand, and hence ordinary reasons to believe in Lefty. That Lefty is a *redundant* cause of my hand-warming is neither here nor there, since Lefty is still a *bona fide* cause of it. Merricks, of course, disagrees. He disagrees that we have ordinary reasons to think that *any* composite objects are *bona fide* causes things, because he holds that (A) establishes that we have no ordinary reasons to believe in any composite objects, and *hence* no ordinary reasons to believe that any composite object is ever a *bona fide* cause of anything. But if (A) lacks justification—and I've argued that it does—then that argument fails.

3. The Curious Case of MO

So far, I've only considered Merricks's argument for the claim that we have no ordinary reasons to believe that Pair (or Lefty or Righty or S or L or T or. . . .) exists. But he argues for a stronger conclusion than this, namely that Pair does *not* exist (and neither do Lefty nor . . .):

> My philosophical reason for denying that Pair exists has two stages. The first is an 'Ockham's razor'-type principle: We should deny the existence of those alleged physical objects that would be, of necessity, wholly causally redundant, especially if we have no good ordinary reasons to believe in such objects. The second is that—as argued above—we have no good ordinary reasons to believe in physical objects that are (of necessity or otherwise) wholly causally redundant.
>
> (139)

The argument of the previous section concluded that we should not endorse this last claim, namely (A). But that leaves the first stage of Merricks's argument relatively unscathed (only relatively, however, because I've argued that we shouldn't endorse the bit that comes after 'especially'—but let's ignore that).

Is the first stage of Merricks's argument—the wielding of the 'Ockham's razor'-type principle that we should *deny* the existence of wholly causally redundant objects—compelling? In fact, Merricks does not attempt to defend this principle directly; instead, he relies on the analogy with his mysterious object O (which, as before, I'll refer to as 'MO')—the purported object that overdetermines the boiling of the kettle and keeping the rug dry, and yet of which neither the kettle nor the roof is a part. MO, like Lefty, is essentially a mere overdeterminer: if it exists, it is, of necessity, a wholly redundant cause.

Merricks is right, I think, to claim that we have good *philosophical* reasons to deny that MO exists. The question is, what are those reasons? Merricks's answer is that those reasons include the fact that MO is, of necessity, wholly causally redundant. I disagree. MO *is*, of course—if it exists—of necessity wholly causally redundant. But we have perfectly good reasons to deny that MO exists without appealing to this particular feature of MO.

MO is stipulatively defined *purely* in terms of its effects: there is no *more* to MO's essence than its having those effects. By contrast, Pair, Lefty, and Righty are not *merely* essentially mere overdeterminers of their various effects. Lefty is (let's assume) essentially an instance of a medium-sized dry good. (Maybe Lefty has other essential features; maybe it's essentially a glove, for example. But let's set that question aside.) Medium-sized dry goods in turn have at least one essential feature: they *have spatial location*.

What about MO? Well, the stove is not a part of MO, and neither is the roof. So it would seem that MO is not located where the stove and roof are. Similarly for all the other objects whose effects are also redundantly caused by MO. MO would appear to lack any spatial location whatsoever, since, were it to have a location it would, presumably, at least displace some air molecules and hence fail to be causally redundant, and it is part of MO's essence that it is wholly causally redundant. So MO has no spatial location—*it isn't anywhere*—and yet it is a *bona fide* cause of some familiar events, such as the kettle boiling. Is MO supposed to be an abstract object or a concrete object? I claim: we have good philosophical reasons for denying that abstract objects are *bona fide* causes of kettles boiling. We also have good philosophical reasons for denying that there are any concrete objects that aren't anywhere. So we have good philosophical reasons to deny that MO exists.

Merricks, of course, accepts that there are *other* philosophical reasons to believe that MO does not exist, aside from the fact that it is essentially a mere causal overdeterminer (139). My counter-claim is that the fact that MO is essentially a mere causal overdeterminer does not, in itself, constitute so much as *a* philosophical reason to believe that MO doesn't exist.[5] That we have good philosophical reasons not to believe in MO, then, does not give us any good reasons not to believe in Lefty, which (if it exists) is different to MO in various salient ways, not least of which is the fact that it has spatial location.

4. The Two-Headed Beast and Other Mereological Monstrosities

At the end of §2, I claimed—admittedly without argument—that we have ordinary reasons to believe that things like gloves and baseballs exist, because we have grounds for thinking that they are *bona fide* causes. One might wonder, then, whether the same goes for any old mereological sum, however gerry-mandered and arbitrary-seeming—which will, it would seem, be a *bona fide* cause in just the way that Lefty is, since it will inherit its (admittedly redundant, but no less *bona fide* for that) causal status from whatever composes it.

Suppose Trenton and I together carry a couch, or stand on the scales, or leap about. Is there an object composed of the two of us, with two heads, two livers, four hands, and a weight of over three hundred pounds? Let's call this monstrous fusion of the two of us the Two-Headed Beast, or Beast for short. Beast, if it exists, causes a lot of things: it causes changes in the couch's location; it causes the scales to register over three hundred pounds; it causes you to experience its wild leaping; and much else besides. Beast's causing of all these phenomena is entirely redundant but nonetheless *bona fide*: *qua* causal explanation of the number displayed on the scales, for example, the explanation that appeals to Beast is no worse than one that appeals to just me and Trenton individually (which in turn is no worse than the one that appeals to just all of Trenton's undetached body parts and all of my undetached body parts, and so on). So perhaps I am committed to saying that we have good ordinary reasons—in the absence of any good reason to think otherwise that don't also apply to Lefty and its ilk—to believe that Beast exists. And not just Beast; we have equally good reasons to believe in an object composed of the Sun and my left foot; *Guernica* and the speck of dust on my computer screen; and so on.

Obviously, that sounds weird: it fails to accord with our common-sense ontology, according to which Lefty and Righty exist but Beast doesn't. (Or maybe not: one might think—as Lewis does (1986: 213) that common sense merely ignores such mereological monstrosities as Beast rather than being decisively committed to their non-existence.) In the current context, however, we are according consonance with common-sense ontology, or lack of it, no epistemic weight at all. If we were, then we would thereby have excellent reasons to believe in Lefty and Righty that have nothing to do with their causal status. Recall that on Merricks's view, our *only* ordinary reasons for believing in Lefty and Righty are causal reasons. If we're assuming, then, that consonance with common-sense ontology provides no grounds for believing in Lefty, we are entitled to assume also that lack of consonance with common-sense ontology provides no grounds for *dis*believing in Beast. So the fact that it sounds weird to say that we have grounds for believing in Beast and its ilk is, in the current context, no objection to that claim.

4.1. Common-Sense Ontology and Real Patterns

Let's grant that a reasonable degree of consonance with common-sense ontology is not an adequacy constraint on a philosophical theory. (I'm inclined to think that it is, but let's leave that aside.) It would nonetheless be nice if most of our ordinary beliefs about the world didn't turn out to be false. Is there *any* hope that a philosophical theory of what there is might deliver this pleasing result?

Well, let's get back to basics. The question Merricks and I are interested in is this: do composite objects—objects that are wholly constituted by smaller objects or *parts*—exist, and, if so, which ones? There are various options on the table. One is full-blown *nihilism*: the claim that *no* composite objects exist, and hence that the only objects that exist are partless simples. Or one might endorse a kind of *mitigated* nihilism: perhaps, as Merricks argues (2001: Ch.4), *persons* and other conscious beings exist, and such beings are composite objects; but, because they aren't causally redundant, we have grounds for believing in them). A second option—Merricks's view, as outlined in §VI of his contribution to this volume and suggested in his 2001 text (115)—is more nuanced: it might be that *some* other composite objects exist, because it might turn out that there is some smallest composite object that we need to believe in if we are to causally explain, say, hand-warming. All of these positions rule out the existence not only of mereological monstrosities, but also all (or nearly all) of the elements of common-sense ontology: tables, gloves, and so on. All we have, when it comes to such entities, is particles (or whatever the smallest unit we need to believe in is) arranged table-wise, glove-wise, and so on—and two-headed-beast-wise, come to that.

On the other end of the spectrum, we have *universalism*—the view that, wherever we have two objects (me and Trenton, say), we have a third object: the mereological sum of those objects (in this case, Beast). So not only Beast but the object composed of the Sun and my left foot, and so on and so on, all exist.

As we've already seen, neither of these views is at all consonant with common-sense ontology, according to which tables, tigers, and gloves exist but Beast and its ilk don't. Even if we assume that consonance with common-sense ontology should carry no weight in the debate about what exists, it may nonetheless seem rather curious that that debate has come to take this all-or-nothing form. We might, surely, have at least thought that common-sense ontology is a good place to *start*. So why has endorsing that ontology proved to be so spectacularly unpopular?

The answer is that it's generally thought that there is no good answer to the *Special Composition Question* (van Inwagen 1990): what are the circumstances under which two objects compose a third object? The standard way things proceed at this point is as follows. Consider a handful of possible ways of answering the question. For example, we might consider the possibility that *x* and *y* compose *z* if and only if *x* and *y* are in contact, or fastened together, or fused, or whatever (van Inwagen 1990; Markosian 1998). Show that none of those answers work. Conclusion: there is no good answer to the Special Composition Question. Hence (unless we endorse what Markosian calls 'brutal composition'), composition must 'occur' either always (universalism) or never (nihilism)—or, if we can make some principled exceptions, as both van Inwagen and Merricks do, we can do so only in very circumscribed circumstances.[6]

What this debate presupposes, of course, is that there is a single *composition relation*—one that equally binds Lefty and Righty together as Pair, the members of a football team together as (say) the Liverpool team, various molecules of water together as the Mediterranean, and so on. Some philosophers have denied that we should accept this assumption (Sanford 1993; Thomasson 2007: Ch.7), claiming instead that we should ask instead 'such manageable substitution instances as 'When is there some ship such that the planks compose the ship?' or "When is there some fort such that the rocks compose the fort?" and so on' (Thomasson 2007: 130). But this kind of approach, as Thomasson seems to accept (2007: §10.3) and Jonathan Schaffer urges (2009: §3.2), is apt to end up in the same place as universalism. After all, I can perfectly easily define, say, the sum of a ship and a fort as a *shipfort* and ask the question, 'When is there some shipfort such that the planks and rocks compose a shipfort?'. So if we're after an answer to the Special Composition Question that discriminates between Lefty and Beast, this kind of piecemeal approach won't appear to do the trick—at least, not on its own.

Here's another question we might ask. *Why* does common-sense ontology countenance some composite objects (Lefty, say) but not others (Beast)? We can plausibly assume that there is some kind of broadly evolutionary explanation for at least some aspects of common-sense ontology, to do with the basic need to stay alive and reproduce. (If there's a tiger-shaped collection of particles, or whatever, in the vicinity of you and your family, it's pretty useful to be able to shout 'Tiger!', as opposed to 'Collection of simples arranged . . . oh dear, too late!'.) Common-sense ontology is incontrovertibly *useful*.

But now we can sensibly ask: *why* is common-sense ontology useful in the way that it undoubtedly is? Why are tigers and tables useful elements in our ontology, but Beast and other mereological monstrosities aren't? A pretty obvious first pass at an answer at this point would be that the collections of particles (or whatever) that make it into our common-sense ontology exhibit certain kinds of features—perhaps such as integrity and stability over time— that *make* them the kinds of thing it's useful to be able to track over time. Terry the Tiger, for example, is a good candidate for existence.[7] His behaviour is reasonably predictable because there are plenty of pretty serviceable generalisations about tigers that we either know or would know if we spent enough time investigating tigers. For much of the time, many of Terry's parts do not operate entirely independently of each other, as when he breaks into a run having spotted a lone gazelle, slurps some water thanks to interaction between various body parts (head, tongue, etc.) and his brain, and so on. We can ask—and, in the right circumstances, come up with an answer that has a good chance of being true—questions such as, 'What would have happened if Terry had been twenty feet further away from the gazelle?'

Perhaps we can also ask what would have happened if there had been no particles arranged Terry-wise in the location at which there are actually particles arranged Terry-wise, and instead there had been some particles arranged Terry-wise twenty feet further away from the particles arranged gazelle-wise—and give it the same answer (suitably translated into language that doesn't imply the existence of Terry or the gazelle). But if to be an object just *is* to exhibit the kind of stability, cohesion, organisation, or whatever that I'm vaguely gesturing towards here, then the fact that we can ask and answer *that* question does not in the least undermine the claim that *Terry* exists. That some particles arranged Terry-wise (if such there be) exhibit such stability, cohesion or whatever is, precisely, the grounds for committing ourselves to the existence of Terry.

Beast, by contrast, exhibits no such integrity or stability. There are no interesting generalisations about two-headed bi-people. For the most part—that is, apart from those rare occasions when we are carrying a couch or standing on the scales together—Trenton and I operate pretty much entirely independently of one another: the extent of co-ordination between those of Beast's parts that compose me and those that compose Trenton would (were Beast to exist) be extremely limited.

This proposal is, of course, incredibly sketchy. For what it's worth, it's in the same ballpark as a rather less sketchy account offered by Don Ross (2000) and Ladyman, Ross and Collier (2007), developed from a position of Dennett's (1991) concerning the ontology of folk psychology—the ontology of beliefs, desires, and so on. As Ross very succinctly sums up the view: 'to be is to be a real pattern' (2000: 161).

The suggestion, then, is not that we should accept common-sense ontology because something's being an element of common-sense ontology is, in itself, grounds for thinking that it exists. Rather, the suggestion is that common-sense ontology, by and large, tracks real, objective patterns, and *that* is what vindicates it—or at least to a great extent vindicates it. Terry, Lefty, and Beast are equally *bona fide* causes, if they exist. But Beast does not constitute an objective pattern of the required kind, and hence we have grounds for denying that Beast exists. Of course, it's an empirical question to what extent, exactly, common-sense ontology would thereby be vindicated. I'm not at all sure about Pair, for example—which is why the earlier part of this chapter focussed on Lefty. My own pairs of gloves, if they exist at all, exhibit barely any more stability or integrity than does Beast—a fact to which my ever-growing collection of unmatching single gloves attests.

Notes

1. Pre-empting causes are often also thought of as 'redundant' causes (Lewis 2000), but I shall ignore pre-emption since it is only overdetermination that is relevant to the case of ordinary objects.

2. Silver bullets only work on werewolves, apparently. But the silver bullet makes the example work, so let's pretend.
3. See Schaffer 2000, in which Merlin and Morgana appear but in a case of trumping pre-emption. The grounds Schaffer presents for thinking that in *his* example one spell trumps the other do not, by stipulation, apply to my case.
4. Unless, that is, you're prepared to grant that SC2 counts as an 'object' for the purposes of evaluating (A*) and (D)—in which case you don't need the additional part of the story I'm about to give.
5. Admittedly I appealed to MO's causally redundant status in the above argument, but only in order to infer that MO has the features that *do* constitute philosophical reasons not to believe in it, *viz* the combination of *being a bona fide cause* and *not being anywhere*.
6. I hereby register my disapproval of speaking of composition as 'occurring'—as though it's something that *happens* or is brought about by some mysterious metaphysical process.
7. Merricks himself agrees that Terry the Tiger exists, because he holds that conscious composite objects (such as Terry) exhibit top-down causation and hence are not causally redundant. See Merricks 2001: 114–116. But the view sketched here—unlike Merricks's —applies just as much to tables and gloves as it does to tigers.

References

Dennett, D. 1991. "Real Patterns." *The Journal of Philosophy* 88: 27–51.
Ladyman, J., D. Ross, and J. Collier. 2007. "Rainforest Realism and the Unity of Science". In J. Ladyman, D. Ross, J. Collier, and D. Spurrett (eds.), *Every Thing Must Go*, 190–257. Oxford: Oxford University Press.
Lewis, D.K. 1986. *On the Plurality of Worlds.* Malden: Blackwell.
———. 2000. "Causation as Influence." *The Journal of Philosophy* 97: 182–197.
Markosian, N. 1998. "Brutal Composition." *Philosophical Studies* 92: 211–249.
Merricks, T. 2001. *Objects and Persons.* Oxford: Oxford University Press.
Ross, D. 2000. "Rainforest Realism: A Dennettian Theory of Existence". In D. Ross, A. Brook, and D. Thompson (eds.), *Dennett's Philosophy: A Comprehensive Assessment*, 147–168. Cambridge, MA: MIT Press.
Sanford, D. 1993. "The Problem of the Many, Many Composition Questions, and Naïve Mereology." *Nous* 27: 219–228.
Schaffer, J. 2000. "Trumping Pre-Emption." *The Journal of Philosophy* 97: 165–181.
———. 2009. "The Deflationary Metaontology of Thomasson's Ordinary Objects." *Philosophical Books* 50: 142–157.
Thomasson, A. 2007. *Ordinary Objects.* New York: Oxford University Press.
van Inwagen, P. 1990. *Material Beings.* Ithaca, NY: Cornell University Press.

Index